TAJIKI REFERENCE GRAMMAR FOR BEGINNERS

ДАСТУРИ ЗАБОНИ ТОҶИКӢ
БАРОИ НАВОМӮЗ

Nasrullo Khojayori
Насрулло Хоҷаёрӣ
  and
Mikael Thompson
Михаил Томпсон

Library of Congress Cataloging-in-Publication Data

Khojayori, Nasrullo.
  Tajiki : an elementary textbook / Nasrullo Khojayori.
    p. cm.
  Includes bibliographical references and index.
  ISBN 978-1-58901-263-9 (pbk. vol. 1 : alk. paper) --
  ISBN 978-1-58901-264-6 (pbk. vol. 2 : alk. paper) --
  ISBN 978-1-58901-269-1 (pbk. reference grammar : alk. paper)
  1. Tajik language--Textbooks for foreign speakers--English.
  I. Title.
  PK6973.K49 2009
  491'.5782421--dc21
                          2008052593

© *2009 Georgetown University Press.*

This grammar book, as well as other language materials for Central Asian Languages produced by CeLCAR, Indiana University-Bloomington, is supported by a Title-VI grant from the Department of Education

TABLE OF CONTENTS

ACKNOWLEDGEMENTS v

INTRODUCTION vii

CHAPTER 1 Orthography and Phonology
Имло ва овошиносӣ 1

CHAPTER 2 Nominals and Prepositions
Ҳиссаҳои номии нутқ ва пешояндҳо 17

CHAPTER 3 Verbs
Феъл 59

CHAPTER 4 Adverbs and Particles
Зарф ва пасояндҳо 113

CHAPTER 5 Compound and Complex Sentences
Ҷумлаҳои мураккаб ва таркибӣ 123

GLOSSARY
Фарҳанги вожаҳо 147

INDEX
Намояи истилоҳот 165

ACKNOWLEDGEMENTS

Як гули мақсуд дар ин бӯстон,
Чида нашуд бе мадади дӯстон.
— Саъди

*There is no flower in the garden of goals
Which was not grown without help of a friend.*
— Saadi

  This textbook could not have been written without the assistance of many people. First, I am deeply grateful to the two scholars who brought me to the United States and gave me the opportunity to write this book: Dr. William Fierman, Director of the Inner Asian and Uralic National Resource Center, whose love of Central Asia, knowledge of its cultures, and appreciation of the role of the national languages in the formation of national identity make him an incomparable advocate in the United States for the study of their languages and cultures; and Dr. Bill Johnston for his excellent ideas and his deep understanding of second-language pedagogy, which have provided his students invaluable guidance in developing textbooks with authentic materials.
  Second, sincere thanks to Dr. Paul Foster, Director of CeLCAR, for his support and dedication throughout this process and providing all the resources needed to complete this book.
  Third, I offer deep thanks to Dr. Azim Baizoyev for editing the Tajiki text; to Mikael Thompson for cowriting the English text and giving help in all areas of the book's composition, and above all for better explaining Tajiki grammar to native English speakers; and last but far from least to my wife, Farzona Zehni, who was involved in all stages of the book and without whose help the book could not have been written. Also, the practical tasks of writing this book were greatly eased by the unstinting efforts of Alisher Davlatzoda, who provided technical support of every kind. Finally, I would like to thank Tom Tudek, Jim Woods and Sukhrob Karimov for design and illustrations.
  I am also very thankful to all my friends who helped me by providing pictures, videos, audios, and all other assistance. I am especially grateful to Khiromon Baqozoda, Tohiri Safar, Abdulfattoh Shafiev, Nasiba Mirpochoeva, Chris Whitsel, David Gay, and Amin Shohmurodov.

Dr. Nasrullo Khojayori

INTRODUCTION

The Tajiki Reference Grammar has the aim of helping any person learning Tajiki, whether in class or self-study. One of the co-authors began work on it while learning of the language himself, and thus our major consideration has been to write from the perspective of potential learners. We have written it in simple language, but with comprehensive treatment of all major grammatical points of Tajiki, particularly those that might prove difficult for native English speakers. It has been organized in traditional fashion, starting with pronunciation and orthography. Nominals (nouns, pronouns, and adjectives), which are very similar as a group, are discussed next, and then the construction of nominal and prepositional phrases and the simplest forms of equational and existential sentences. The Tajiki verbal system and the construction of simple sentences is discussed next, after which adverbs and other words whose position in a sentence is highly dependent on the surrounding parts of speech are treated. Finally, the basic ways of forming compound and complex sentences are discussed in detail. An important tool for the reader is the index, which has been compiled with an eye to including references to every important mention of Tajiki verb tenses (such as the tenses used in the different kinds of compound and complex sentences), izofat, use of the personal possessive markers as direct and indirect objects, and other topics that run throughout the book, so the learner should refer to the index as well as the table of contents whenever there is a question on a particular topic.

Chapter 1 Orthography and Phonology

1. The Tajiki Alphabet

The Tajiki language used a modified Arabic alphabet from the 8th century until the 1920s. In 1928 the Latin alphabet was adopted but a modified Cyrillic alphabet became the official Tajiki alphabet in 1940. The Cyrillic alphabet used for Tajiki contains a total of 35 letters. Of these, 24 are consonants and 6 (plus **й**, a variant of **и** only used at the end of the word) are vowels, while 4 indicate "yoted (or yotated) letters," *y* [**й**] followed by a vowel. Following is a list of the Tajiki vowels, consonants, and yoted letters in the Cyrillic script.

Vowels: **а, и (й), о, у, ӯ, э (е)**
Consonants: **б, в, г, ғ, д, ж, з, й, к, қ, л, м, н, п, р, с, т, ф, х, ҳ, ч, ҷ, ш, ъ**
Yoted letters: **е, ё, ю, я**

2. Vowels

The six Tajiki vowels can be classified according to their *phonetic features*—that is, the position of the tongue and the rounding of the lips when saying them: front/back, high/mid/low, and rounded/unrounded. Front vowels (**и, э**) are produced when the tongue moves forward during articulation and back vowels (**у, о**) when the tongue moves backward. Mixed or central vowels (**ӯ, а**) are produced when tongue stays in the middle of the mouth. High vowels (**и, у**), mid vowels (**ӯ, о, э**), and the low vowel (**а**) are produced when the height of the tongue is high, mid, and low, respectively. Rounded vowels (**ӯ, у, о**) are produced with rounded lips, while unrounded vowels (**а, и, э**) are pronounced with unrounded or "spread" lips. Unlike English, Tajiki vowels are always "pure" (monophthongs), keeping the same pronunciation throughout: The final *w* sound in *show* or *shoe* does not occur with the Tajiki vowels **о** or **у**, nor does **и** or **э** have the final *y* sound in *see* or *say*.

Table of Vowels

	front	central	back	
high			y	*rounded*
	и			*unrounded*
mid		ӯ	o	*rounded*
	э			*unrounded*
low				*rounded*
		a		*unrounded*

a Central low unrounded. Sounds like *a* in *father*.
и Front high unrounded. Sounds like *ee* in *feet*.
й Pronounced like **и**; used at the end of a word to indicate stress (except in the 2nd singular verb ending).
о Back mid rounded. Sounds like *oa* in *boat*.
у Back high rounded. Sounds like *oo* in *choose*.
ӯ Central mid rounded vowel. Like *u* in *cut* with rounded lips.
э (е) Front mid unrounded vowel. Sounds like *e* in *telegraph*.

The Tajiki vowels can also be divided into two groups according to their length. In this case the number of Tajiki vowels increases to eight because **и** and **у** can be long or short. The difference in length is not indicated in the script.

The short vowels are: **а, и, у**
The long vowels are: **и, у, о, э, ӯ**

3. Consonants

There are twenty-four Tajiki consonants. Sixteen of them fall into pairs that are identical except for voicing. Voicing is the humming or buzzing sound that occurs when the breath passing through the voice box (the *larynx*) causes the vocal cords to vibrate; voiced consonants have voicing and voiceless consonants do not. (To determine whether a consonant is voiced, put your fingers on your voice box and say the sound; if there is a steady buzz of vibrations, the consonant is voiced. Alternatively, cover your ears with your hands and say the consonant. If the consonant is voiced, you should hear a buzz in your ears as you speak; this buzz is the vibration of the vocal cords transmitted through the bones of the neck and head.) For example, in English the sound *s* is voiceless, and *z* is identical except that it is voiced; similarly with *p* and *b*, *t* and *d*, etc.

The Tajiki consonants are listed below as voiced or voiceless, with pairs of consonants differing only in voicing shown.

Voiced consonants: б в д з ж ҷ г ғ - - - м н л р й
Voiceless consonants: п ф т с ш ч к х қ ъ ҳ - - - - -

Voiced consonants are devoiced—that is, they are replaced by their voiceless counterparts—in final position and immediately before voiceless consonants. Similarly, voiceless consonants are voiced, that is, replaced by their voiced counterparts, immediately before voiced consonants. (Note that this applies only to the voiced and voiceless consonants that come in pairs; л, р, й, м, and н, for example, are always voiced.)

Linguists also classify consonants according to their place and manner of articulation. The *place of articulation* is the part of the mouth that is most closed, either by the tongue or the lower lip; the *manner of articulation* indicates how strong the closure is. The specific features of each consonant are given in the following chart.

Бб	[b]	Voiced bilabial stop like *b* in *book, back*. When it occurs at the end of the word or before voiceless consonants it is pronounced voiceless: хуб [хуп], чӯб [чӯп], обкаш [опкаш]
Вв	[v]	Voiced labiodental fricative like *v* in *very, vet*.
Гг	[g]	Voiced velar stop like *g* in *get, good*. It becomes voiceless before voiceless consonants: тагшин [такшин]
Ғғ	[gh]	Voiced velar fricative, rather like the French *r* in *français*, but rougher.
Дд	[d]	Voiced dental stop like *d* in *dot*, but pronounced with the tip of the tongue against the back of the upper front teeth.

Жж	[zh]	Voiced alveo-palatal fricative like *s* in *pleasure*.
Зз	[z]	Voiced alveolar fricative like *z* in *zoo*.
Йй	[y]	Voiced alveolar glide like *y* in *yes, you, boy*.
Кк	[k]	Voiceless velar stop like *k* in *candle, key*. Before voiced consonants it becomes voiced: **токзор** [**тогзор**]
Ққ	[q]	Voiceless uvular stop. Similar to *k* in *coop* or *kook*, but with the tongue much further back towards the throat.
Лл	[l]	Voiced lateral liquid like *l* in *lid, like, lake*.
Мм	[m]	Voiced labial nasal like *m* in *memorial, men, muscle*.
Нн	[n]	Voiced alveolar nasal like *n* in *noun, nerve, name*.
Пп	[p]	Voiceless labial stop like *p* in *spot*. It does not have the aspiration (the heavy burst of air) of the *p* in *post, pack*.
Рр	[r]	Voiced retroflex liquid (flap), somewhat like *r* in English words *run, rule*. Very close to Spanish or Russian *r*.
Сс	[s]	Voiceless dental fricative like *s* if produced in *see, sailor* with the tongue closer to the teeth.
Тт	[t]	Voiceless dental stop like *t* in *take, tune* if produced with the tongue against the upper front teeth.

Фф	[f]	Voiceless labiodental fricative like *f* in *few, female*.
Хх	[kh]	Voiceless uvular fricative like German *ch* in *Bach*, only rougher.
Ҳҳ	[h]	Voiceless glottal fricative like *h* in *hot, hill* and *hate*.
Чч	[ch]	Voiceless alveopalatal affricate like *ch* in *child, chicken*.
Ҷҷ	[j]	Voiced alveopalatal affricate like *j* in *just*.
Шш	[sh]	Voiceless alveopalatal fricative like *sh* in *show, shame, shake*.
ъ	[']	Voiceless glottal stop like the catch in the throat in *uh-oh*.

4. Yoted Letters

In Tajiki, each letter usually represents a single sound, and sounds are generally pronounced the same whether at the beginning, in the middle, or at the end of a word. But because Tajiki borrowed Cyrillic script from Russian there are four letters in Tajiki which follow Russian convention to represent y [й] followed by a vowel:

е = й + э   ю = й + у
ё = й + о   я = й + а

For example:

йак = як   йурт = юрт
йор = ёр   йэлим = елим

The letter **e**, however, is not always a yoted letter. At the beginning of a word it always indicates *ye* [й + э], but in the middle or at the end of a word it indicates *ye* [й + э] following a vowel or a yoted letter and *e* [э] following a consonant.

Compare:
чойе 'some tea'	(**чой** 'tea')
мӯйе 'some hair'	(**мӯй** 'hair')
бӯйе 'some smell, a smell'	(**бӯй** 'smell')
рӯйе 'a face'	(**рӯй** 'face')
марде 'a man'	(**мард** 'man')
зане 'a woman'	(**зан** 'woman')

Therefore in contemporary Tajiki there is a tendency to use the letter **e** to represent only the sound **э** in the middle and final positions. Thus, if we add the suffix **e** to a word like **чой**, it is often written **чойе** instead of **чое**.

5. Changes in Pronunciation (Phonological Rules)

The pronunciations of many Tajiki letters change from how they are described above depending on their position in the word or the sounds next to them. In addition, there are some changes in pronunciation when a suffix is added to a word. In this section, square brackets are used to indicate the pronunciation of the word when it differs from the spelling; thus, [хаф] indicates that the word spelled **ҳафт** 'seven' is pronounced *haf*, not *haft*. Similarly, forms in parentheses are not pronounced as written, but are the "original" or underlying forms of words before changes that make them easier to pronounce.

5.1 Positional Changes

The vowels *a* [а], *u* [у], and *i* [и] are reduced (pronounced weaker) in unstressed syllables. Sometimes they are pronounced rather like the vowels in *cut, wood,* and *pin,* respectively, but often they are reduced to the first vowel (the schwa vowel) in *about* or *around*.

Some voiced consonants are devoiced at the end of a word unless the following word begins with a voiced consonant.

5.2 Changes Conditioned by Other Sounds

a. Assimilation: Some consonants change to become more like following consonants.

1) When *n* [н] precedes a labial consonant (*b* [б], *p* [п], *f* [ф], *v* [в], *m* [м]), it is pronounced *m* [м]:

> танбал > [тамбал] 'lazy'
> шанбе > [шамбе] 'Saturday'

2) Voiced consonants are devoiced when followed by voiceless consonants; similarly, voiceless consonants are voiced when preceding voiced consonants:

> бадтар > [баттар] 'worse'
> гапзанй > [габзанй] 'talking'

b. Deletion (loss): Some sounds are not pronounced in certain circumstances, such as when consonants occur in sequence (a cluster).

1) In clusters of three consonants, the middle consonant is often not pronounced:

> хиштрез > [хишрез] 'brick-maker'
> баландтар > [балантар] 'higher'

However, in some cases a vowel is inserted after the second consonant. (See Section c below, "Insertion").

2) In clusters of two consonants at the end of a word, the last consonant is sometimes not pronounced:

> хафт > [хаф] 'seven'
> хашт > [хаш] 'eight'
> карданд > [кардан] 'they did'

Certain words end in a single consonant that gets doubled (a *geminate* consonant) when a suffix beginning with a vowel is added; these words are identified in this book with the second consonant in parentheses: **син(н)** 'age,' **фан(н)** 'art, science, field of study.'

3) **в** is often deleted between like vowels:

    меравам > [**мерам**] 'I will go'
    мешввам > [**мешам**] 'I will became'

4) **х** is deleted at the end of a word. (However, it is pronounced when a suffix is added.) Also, **ъ** is often deleted between vowels; it is only retained in Arabic words in which it is originally doubled (*geminate*): **фаъол** 'lively.'

    даҳ > [**да**] 'ten'   **даҳум** > [**даҳум**] 'tenth'
    нигоҳ > [**ниго**] 'sight'   **нигоҳи гарм** 'warm glance'
    иттилоот, *plural of* **иттилоъ** 'piece of information'

c. Insertion: In certain circumstances, sounds are added to break up uncomfortable sequences of sounds.

1) In certain cases a vowel is inserted between the second and third consonants of a consonant cluster when forming a compound word (remember that the forms in parentheses are never spoken or written):

    (**мард-кор**) > **мардикор** 'worker'
    (**сохт-мон**) > **сохтумон** 'construction'
    (**шаҳр-ёр**) > **шаҳриёр** 'king'

2) Certain consonants are inserted when two vowels are joined. Most commonly **й** [y] is automatically added (especially between like vowels) and is not always written.

    гушна-анд > [**гушна-й-анд**] **гушнаанд** 'they are hungry'
    ду-ум > [**дуйум**] **дуюм** 'second'

3) Occasionally consonants are added in suffixation:

    (**бозӣ + гар**) > **бозӣ-н-гар** 'player, sportsman'

d. Metathesis: Certain sequences of consonants are not allowed and the order of the consonants is switched in speaking (which is called metathesis). This happens most commonly in Arabic loanwords, which are spelled as in Arabic but pronounced in Tajiki fashion:

қуфл 'lock' > [қулф]
китф 'shoulder' > [кифт]
ҷумъа 'Friday' > [ҷуъма]

6. Syllabification

All syllables in Tajiki contain one and only one vowel. There are as many syllables in a word as there are vowels. Syllables may end in a vowel, a consonant, or two consonants. In Tajiki *no syllables begin with two consonants.* Therefore the syllabic division falls between the two consonants of a two-consonant cluster and between the second and third consonants of a three-consonant cluster. (Since yoted letters begin with a consonant, there is a syllable break just before any yoted letter inside a word: **бир-ён** 'fried,' **тай-ёр** 'ready')

Syllable types in traditional Tajiki words

Syllable	As a complete word	Within the word
V	ӯ 'he, she, it'	а-нор 'pomegranate'
CV	бо 'with,' ва 'and'	ка-буд 'blue'
VC	об 'water,' аз 'from'	аб-рӯ 'eyebrow'
CVC	шаб 'night,' кор 'work'	хан-да 'laughed'
VCC	абр 'cloud,' ишқ 'love'	асп-бон 'stable-man'
CVCC	гӯшт 'meat,' корд 'knife'	сахт-кор 'hard-working'

7. Stress

Most Tajiki words have one primary stress. Usually the stress falls on either the first syllable (in finite verb forms) or the last (in nouns and nounlike words). Unstressed words and meaningful units (called *morphemes* by linguists) tend to fuse with neighboring stressed words without affecting their stress; these are called *clitics* in Tajiki. In the following examples, the stressed syllable is underlined. (Note that a number of words and forms included below are not discussed further in the book.)

7.1 Words with stress on the last syllable.

This is the biggest stress group in Tajiki, including all nouns (except some proper nouns), adjectives, most pronouns, nonconjugated forms of the verb (such as the lexical or dictionary form), and several classes of adverbs. This group can be divided into following grammatical subgroups:

a. All nouns in their lexical form:
саҳро 'field'
хониш 'reading'
мардум 'people'
пахтакор 'cotton-grower'
пахтачинӣ 'picking of cotton'
сафедӣ 'whiteness, yogurt'
донишҷӯ 'student'
савдогар 'merchant'

b. All adjectives:
сафед 'white'
оҳанин 'iron, made of iron'
бисёрошёна 'multi-storey'
қадбаланд 'tall'
абрӯкамон 'with arched brows'

c. All numbers:
ҳазор 'thousand'
панҷсад 'five hundred'
ҳафтум 'seventh'
сеяк 'a third'
дувоздаҳ 'twelve'
ҳафтод 'seventy'
сесад 'three hundred'
нуздаҳ 'nineteen'
шонздаҳум 'sixteenth'
чоряк 'a fourth'
хонаи панҷум 'the fifth house'
ҳазор аскар 'a thousand soldiers'

Note: *if the numbers* дусад *'two hundred,'* сесад *'three hundred,'* чорсад 'four hundred,' **панҷсад** 'five hundred,' **шашсад** 'six hundred,' **ҳафтсад** 'seven hundred,' **ҳаштсад** 'eight hundred,' and **нӯҳсад** 'nine hundred' occur in compound numbers, the stress moves to the first syllable of these words: **сесаду бист** 'three hundred and twenty.'

The nominal parts of speech can take following grammatical

d. Some pronouns in the following groups:

1) *interrogative*:	2) *demonstrative*:
киҳо 'who'	**ҳамин** 'this one'
чиҳо 'what'	**ҳамон** 'that one'
чандум, кадом, кадомин 'which'	**чунин** 'such, like this'
	чунон 'such, like that'

3) *indefinite*:	4) *reciprocal*:
кадом 'which'	**дигар** 'other'
ягон 'some'	**якдигар** 'each other'
фалон 'someone, such-and-such a person'	**ҳамдигар** 'each other'
фалонӣ 'some person'	
чандин 'several'	

e. All infinitives:

хондан 'to read,'   **дидан** 'to see'   **хӯрдан** 'to eat'

f. All participial forms:

1) *past participle*:	2) *present participle*:
хонда 'read'	**раванда** 'going'
навишта 'written'	**шунаванда** 'listener'
баромада 'gone out'	**бинанда** 'watcher'
гирифта 'taken'	**гиранда** 'taker'
омада 'come'	**хонанда** 'reader'
дода 'given'	

3) *agent past participle*:	4) *future participle*:
мерафтагӣ 'the one who will go'	**рафтанӣ** *in*
меомадагӣ 'the one who will come'	**Ман дирӯз рафтанӣ будам,**
медидагӣ 'the one who will see'	'I wanted to go yesterday.'
мехондагӣ 'the one who will read'	

g. **Verbal adjectives:**

бозикун<u>он</u> 'playfully'
табассумкун<u>он</u> 'smilingly'

роҳрав<u>он</u> 'while going'
сӯҳбаткун<u>он</u> 'while conversing'

h. **Some adverbs of the following groups:**

1) *manner:*	2) *time:*	3) *place*
дарело<u>на</u> 'bravely' ху<u>ш</u>ҳоло<u>на</u> 'happily' мардо<u>на</u> 'masculine' оҳис<u>та</u> 'quickly' паснок<u>ӣ</u> 'backwards'	рӯзо<u>на</u> 'in the daytime, daily' шабо<u>на</u> 'in the nighttime, nightly' бегоҳ<u>ӣ</u> 'in the evening' пагоҳ<u>ӣ</u> 'in the morning' нисфирӯз<u>ӣ</u> 'noontime' пешин<u>ӣ</u> 'at noon'	по<u>ён</u> 'at the bottom' бе<u>рун</u> 'outside' қа<u>фо</u> 'back'

indicators. These are all enclitics, so the stress remains on the last syllable of the root word:

a) *izofat:*	b) *direct object marker* **-ро**:	c) *indefinite article* **-e**:
хо<u>наи</u> **ман** 'my house' ки<u>тоби</u> **нав** 'new book' па<u>дари</u> **Шумо** 'your father'	ки<u>то</u>бро 'the book' <u>он</u>ро 'that, him, her, it'	ки<u>то</u>бе 'a book' қа<u>ла</u>ме 'a pencil'

d) *personal possessive markers* (-ам, -ат, -аш, -амон, -атон, -ашон):	e) *conjunction* **-у (-ю)**:
ки<u>то</u>бам 'my book' ки<u>то</u>бат 'your book' ки<u>то</u>башон 'their book'	ки<u>то</u>бу қалам 'book and pencil' <u>бо</u>ю камба<u>ғал</u> 'rich and poor'

7.2 Words with strees on the first syllable.

This stress group is also very large in Tajiki and includes all conjugated or finite verb forms (verbs used in a complete sentence showing tense). This group includes the following types of words:

a. Some pronouns:

1) *interrogative*:	2) *demonstrative*:
чй хел 'how' **чй гуна** 'what kind' **чй навъ** 'what kind' **чй тарз** 'what kind'	**ин хел** 'this way' **он хел** 'that way' **инчунин** 'like this' **ончунин** 'like that' **ҳамчунин** 'also; also this way' **ҳамчунон** 'also; also that way'
3) *intensive* (**таъйинй**)	4) *indefinite*:
ҳама 'all' **ҳар як** 'each one' **ҳар кадом** 'everyone'	**баъзе** 'some' **ким-кӣ** 'someone' **ким-чӣ** 'something' **ким-кадом** 'some such'

b. Conjugated forms of simple verbs:

1) *simple past*:	2) *past imperfect*:	3) *present perfect*:
гирифтам 'I took' **хондам** 'I read' **дидам** 'I saw' **омадам** 'I came' **хандидам** 'I laughed'	**медидам** 'I used to see' **медидагистам** 'maybe I will see' **мехондам** 'I was reading'	**дидаам** 'I have seen' **гирифтаам** 'I have taken'
4) *habitual reportative*:		5) *imperative*:
Ӯ падарашро ҳар рӯз медидааст, 'He used to see his father every day.' **Ӯ ҳар рӯз аз нонво нон мехаридааст,** 'He used to buy bread from the baker every day.'		**хононед** 'make him read' **нависонед** 'make him write' **оред** 'take' **баред** 'carry'

c. Adverbs:

1) manner:	2) time:	3) quantity and degree:
даррав 'immediately' **нохост** 'suddenly' **беихтиёр** 'unwillingly'	**дирӯз** 'yesterday' **имрӯз** 'today' **дина** 'yesterday' **фардо** 'tomorrow' **пасфардо** 'day after tomorrow' **порсол** 'last year' **дархол** 'immediately' **порина** 'last year' **навакак** 'just now, recently'	**ин қадар** 'this much' **он қадар** 'that much' **як қадар** 'some' **андак** 'a little'

d. Some conjunctions:

1) reason:	2) coordinating conjunction:	3) concessive:
зеро, зеро ки, чаро ки, чунки 'because'	**аммо, вале** 'but' **лекин** 'however' **набошад** 'if so'	**харчи** 'everything' **харчанд** 'although' **харчанд ки** 'although that'
4) time:	5) similarity:	
вақте ки, даме ки 'when'	**гӯё ки** 'as if'	

e. Some sentence particles (ҳиссача):

1) demonstrative:	2) affirmative:
ана 'that one there' **мана** 'this one here'	**оре** 'yes' **бале** 'yes' **майлаш** 'okay'
3) interrogative:	4) modal:
оё 'question word' **наход** 'really' **наход ки** 'really'	**кошкӣ** 'would that' **мабодо** 'beware, I fear' **шояд** 'should, might' **бигзор** 'let it be that' **канӣ** 'where'

f. All interjections:

хӯше 'hush!, don't say that!'　　хоппа 'catch!'
ӯбо 'uh-oh!'　　ало 'hello, hey'
бораколло 'good job!'　　ура 'hooray!'
ҳайфо 'alas!'　　ӯҳӯ 'a-ha!'

g. Arabic words and phrases:

алқисса 'in conclusion'　　филчумла 'as well'
минбаъд 'hereinafter'　　лоақал 'at least'

When a word is suffixed the stress moves to the suffix. (This is the feature that distinguishes suffixes and enclitics in Tajiki.)

All auxiliary verbs are unstressed. In the negative form of the verb, stress moves onto the negative prefix на-: на́хондам 'I didn't read,' кор на́кардам 'I didn't work,' тамом на́шудааст 'it hasn't been finished,' дида на́мешавад 'he won't be seen.'

7.3 Unstressed Words and Morphemes

Unstressed words and morphemes, or clitics, are divided into two groups: *proclitics* and *enclitics*. Proclitics fuse onto the following word, while enclitics fuse onto the preceding word.

a. Proclitics:

1) *simple prepositions*:	2) *conjunctions*:
аз 'from'	чи...чи 'whether...or'
бо 'with'	ё...ё 'either...or'
ба 'to'	ва 'and'
бе 'without'	
бар 'through'	
то 'until'	
дар 'in, at'	
аз хона 'from home'	
бо қалам 'with a pencil'	
бе заҳмат 'without a burden'	
дар роҳ 'on the road'	
то Душанбе 'until/as far as Dushanbe'	

b. Enclitics:
1) verb endings: **-ам, -й, -ад, -ем, -ед, -анд**
2) personal possessive markers: **-ам, -ат, -аш, -амон, -атон, -ашон**
3) predicate endings ('to be'): **-ам, -й, аст, -ем, -ед, -анд**
4) auxiliary verbs: **будан, шудан, намудан**, etc.
5) particles: **-ро, -барин, -боз, -катӣ/қатӣ, -чӣ, -а, -дия, -да, -е, -ку, -куя**
6) conjunctions: **-у (-ю, -ву)**
7) subordinating conjunction: **ки**
8) izofat: **-и**
9) indefinite article: **-е (шахсе** 'some person,' **марде** 'some man')

Chapter 2   Nominals and Prepositions

Nouns, pronouns, and adjectives are grammatically similar in English and Tajiki. Unlike French, Spanish, German, Russian, Latin, or Greek, for example, Tajiki does not have grammatical gender even in pronouns: **ӯ** and **вай** both mean 'he' or 'she' indifferently. Again like English, adjectives do not agree with nouns in number. Similarly, unlike German, Russian, Latin, and Greek, for example, Tajiki has only one distinct case, the definite accusative **-ро** (indicating a definite direct object); other grammatical functions are indicated by prepositions and word position.

On the other hand, pronouns and nouns are more similar to each other in Tajiki than in English (most pronouns form plurals just like nouns do, for example).

First, nouns, pronouns and adjectives will be discussed individually, as well as suffixes used to convert adjectives to nouns and vice versa, then the formation of noun phrases and izofat (which is used to indicate possession and modification by an adjective) will be discussed; in this respect Tajiki and English are quite different and the use of izofat should be learned before proceeding. Once the use of izofat to form noun phrases is understood, prepositions, prepositional phrases, and equational and existential sentences in the present tense are discussed, after which the student can proceed to the section on verbs.

1. Nouns

As in English, Tajiki nouns essentially name people, animals, places, things, and ideas (qualities and abstractions): For example, **мард** 'man,' **зан** 'woman' **бача** 'child,' **гурба** 'cat,' **асп** 'horse,' **шаҳр** 'city,' **дарё** 'river,' **ҷангал** 'forest,' **китоб** 'book,' **дарахт** 'tree,' **дил** 'heart,' **хушбахтӣ** 'happiness,' **бузургӣ** 'height.' Tajiki nouns can be singular or plural; except for certain types of nouns borrowed from Arabic, the plural of a noun is formed from the singular with a suffix.

The basic form of the noun is used as the subject of a sentence, but as with English this form does not change if the noun is used as the object of a preposition. Moreover, there is no special possessive form like English *man's*, *car's*, or *dogs'*; instead, the noun that is possessed takes a special marker, the izofat (see Section 5.2 below).

When a noun is used as a direct object, it takes the ending **-ро** after any plural suffixes if it is definite (roughly, if its English equivalent takes the definite article *the*); otherwise, the noun usually takes no ending. In fact, the issue of when a noun is definite in Tajiki is quite complex and will be discussed in some detail in Chapter 3, Section 2. The form **-ро** is literary or formal; in colloquial speech the form **-а** is used after consonants and **-я** (northern dialects) or **-ра** (southern dialects) after vowels:

Formal	*Colloquial (N)*	*Colloquial (S)*	
китобро	**китоба**	**китоба**	'book'
хонаро	**хоная**	**хонара**	'house'

Китоба гир! 'Take the book!'
Хоная бин! 'See the house!'
Косара те! 'Give (me) the bowl!'

Note that in older Persian, **-ро** could indicate either a direct or an indirect object; the usage indicating an indirect object survives in some set phrases (**Худоро шукр**, 'Thanks to the Lord') and in poetry.

Similarly, in English indefiniteness is usually shown by the indefinite articles *a/an* in the singular and *some* in the plural. In Tajiki a simple noun or noun phrase can be made indefinite with the clitic **-е**, which is added after any plural suffix and before **-ро**; it never takes the stress.

In addition, a few particles that can follow the noun or noun phrase are written as separate words even though they are enclitics (and thus fuse with the preceding word and do not take stress). The most important are **ҳам/низ** 'also' (**низ** literary; they immediately follow the noun phrase they modify. Frequently in colloquial speech **ҳам** loses the **ҳ** and automatically adds a **й** in pronunciation after a vowel, and so becomes homophonous with the personal possessive marker **-ам** 'my') and **барин** 'like, resembling.'

1.1 Plural formations

In Tajiki the most common plural is formed by adding the suffix **-ҳо** to the end of the noun; this suffix can be added to all Tajiki nouns and takes the stress.

қалам 'pencil'   **қаламҳо** 'pencils'
мард 'a man'   **мардҳо** 'men'

The **ҳ** in the suffix **-ҳо** is not pronounced after consonants in the colloquial language:

китоб 'a book' > **китобҳо** [китобо] 'books'
хона 'a house' > **хонаҳо** [хонаҳо] 'houses'

However, there are other plural forms for certain groups of nouns. First, the plural marker **-он** is used with animate nouns and some inanimate nouns.

1. **people and occupations:** **муаллимон** 'teachers,' **рассомон** 'artists,' **занон** 'women,' **мардон** 'men,' **одамон** 'people';
2. **parts of the human body that come in pairs:** **дастон** 'hands,' **лабон** 'lips,' **чашмон** 'eyes';
3. **nouns with the suffixes -зор, -сор, -бор:** **лолазорон** 'tulip gardens,' **кӯҳсорон** 'mountains,' **ҷӯйборон** 'canals';
4. **names of plants, trees, and their parts:** **дарахтон** 'trees,' **баргон** 'leaves,' **муғҷагон** 'buds,' **шохон** 'branch';
5. **names of celestial bodies:** **ситорагон** 'stars,' **ахтарон** 'stars,' **сайёрагон** 'planets';
6. **names of time units:** **шабон** 'nights,' **рӯзон** 'days,' **баҳорон** 'springs, in springtime.'

This suffix has three variants: **-гон, -вон, -ён.**

1. After consonants -<u>он</u> is used: **мардон** 'men,' **занон** 'women,' **одамон** 'people,' **дарахтон** 'trees.'
2. After the vowel <u>а</u> (including the yoted vowel **я**), the suffix -<u>гон</u> is used: **ҳамсоягон** 'neighbors,' **бачагон** 'children,' **набарагон** 'grandchildren.'

3. After the vowels й and о and yoted ё, the suffix -ён is used: **бобоён** 'grandfathers, old men,' **кӯҳистониён** 'mountain people.'

4. After the vowel у, the suffix -вон is used: **бонувон** 'ladies,' **ҳиндувон** 'Hindus, Indians.'

In addition, a number of words borrowed from Arabic take other Arabic plural forms.

a) The dual suffix -айн. This suffix indicates two of a noun in Arabic. Only two words that take this suffix are common in Tajiki, both with the meaning of 'both of a pair':

  тарафайн 'both sides'   **волидайн** 'both parents'

b) The plural suffix -от (very common).

  маълум 'something known'   **маълумот** 'information'
  иттилоъ 'piece of information'   **иттилоот** 'information'
  воқеа 'event'   **воқеот** 'events'
  ворид 'entering'   **воридот** 'imports'
  содир 'publication'   **содирот** 'exports'

The suffix **-от** is used mostly with Arabic words, but it is taken by a few Tajiki nouns:

  деҳа 'village'   **деҳот** 'villages'
  сабза 'green things'   **сабзавот** 'vegetables'
  боғ 'garden'   **боғот** 'gardens'
  навишта   **навиштаҷот**
  'something written'   'compositions, writings, oeuvre'

c) The plural suffix -ин (less common).

  муаллим 'teacher'   **муаллимин** 'teachers'
  мусофир 'traveler'   **мусофирин** 'travelers'

d) Broken plural forms. Arabic *broken plurals* are very common in Tajiki; they are formed by retaining the consonants in the singular and inserting different vowels between them. Thus, the broken plural of **ҳарф** '*letter (of an alphabet)*' is **ҳуруф**. There are a large number of patterns for broken plurals in Arabic, some followed by only a handful of nouns, others by almost all nouns of a particular shape. Arabic broken plurals are named in traditional Arabic grammar by giving the general form of the plural—the consonants are replaced with **ф, ъ**, and **л**, respectively, and the appropriate vowels are inserted. The most common classes of broken plurals are:

1. **афъол** (*afʻol*)
    хабар '(piece of) news'   **ахбор** 'news'
    тараф 'side'   **атроф** 'sides'
    шахс 'person'   **ашхос** 'people'
2. **фуъъол** (*fuʻʻol*)
    ҳоким 'mayor'   **ҳукком** 'mayors'
3. **мафоъил** (*mafoʻil*)
    мактаб 'school'   **макотиб** 'schools'
    маҳфил 'club, group'   **маҳофил** 'clubs, groups'
    машғала 'noise'   **машоғил** 'noises'

Broken plurals, especially of the less common patterns, are used more commonly in literary Tajiki than in colloquial speech.

1.2 Use of the plural

Plurality is not shown when a noun is modified by a numeral: **одамон** 'people,' **ду одам** 'two people.' Numerals are often followed by one of a number of different *classifiers* (also called *numeratives*), especially when modifying inanimate nouns. The most common classifiers are: **нафар** for people (never used with **кас** or **одам**), **сар** for animals, **дона** for things, **адад** for commercial items, and **то (та)** for any noun. Other classifiers are usually measure words like **кило** 'kilogram,' **метр** 'meter,' and **литр** 'liter,' but also include such words indicating types or quantities of things as **бандча** 'bundle' and **халта** 'bag, sack.' Words for units of time and distance do not need classifiers: **ду соат** 'two hours.'

Plurality is used somewhat differently in Tajiki and English. In English, plurals are used for all nouns that name more than one object mentioned in a sentence; however, in Tajiki plurals are not often used for inanimate nouns. Moreover, in English plural nouns are often used for general groups or categories of things (*generic*), but not for abstract nouns: *People like him, it's fun to hunt mushrooms, stones are good for building a solid house.* In Tajiki, this is only true of animate nouns (often including plants, especially large ones like **дарахтон** 'trees'): **одамон** 'people,' **сагҳо** 'dogs.'

For inanimate nouns, on the other hand, Tajiki more commonly than English uses the singular form, which in fact for inanimate nouns should be seen rather as indeterminate in number. (Plural forms of inanimate nouns are of course used when it is necessary to emphasize that more than one thing is being disussed.) For example: **себ** 'an apple, apples,' **себҳо** 'apples,' **себе/як себ** 'an apple.'

In both English and Tajiki, abstract nouns very rarely occur in the plural, in which case they refer to different *types* of a quality or abstraction.

Just as in English, nouns can be joined using conjunctions, the most important of which in Tajiki are **ва** and **-у** 'and,' **ё** 'or,' and **не... не** 'neither...nor'; these can also be used with pronouns and adjectives. Usually they only occur before the last word in a series.

2. Pronouns

Pronouns are words that stand in for or refer to nouns, such as *I, she, who, what, these,* and *those.* There are four types of pronouns in Tajiki, personal, interrogative, demonstrative, and indefinite pronouns; personal pronouns include reflexive, reciprocal, and intensive pronouns (see Section 5.3 below). Indefinite pronouns will be discussed in detail later with indefinite adverbs; the other three types of pronouns are discussed below. (English also has what are called possessive pronouns: *My, mine, whose,* etc. In Tajiki, possession is indicated the same way for nouns and pronouns; there are no distinct possessive pronouns. See Section 5.2 on izofat below.)

2.1 Personal pronouns

Personal pronouns stand in for a noun and indicate its relation to the speaker and hearer of a sentence. As in English, Tajiki personal pronouns are singular or plural and indicate three persons: First person includes the speaker (*I, we*), second person the hearer but not the speaker (*you*), and third person refers to neither the speaker nor the hearer (*he, she, it, they*).

	Singular	Plural
1st	ман 'I'	мо (моён) 'we'
2nd	ту (Шумо) 'you' (*sg.*)	шумо (Шумоён) 'you' (*pl.*)
3rd	ӯ, вай, он 'he, she, it'	онҳо (уно), вайҳо (ваё) 'they'

Unlike English, these forms of the personal pronouns are used in all cases, whether as subject or object of a sentence, object of a preposition, or possessive; the direct object of the personal pronouns is formed regularly by adding **-ро**, except that the direct object of **ман** is **маро**.

Tajiki does not distinguish gender grammatically; **ӯ, вай**, and **он** each mean *he, she,* or *it*. The first two can be used almost interchangeably for people or things (**вай** is more common and **ӯ** more literary), while **он** tends to be used more for inanimate objects. In colloquial Tajiki, **онҳо** and **вайҳо** are pronounced **уно** and **ваё**.

Шумо is often used as a polite form of addressing someone, in which case it is capitalized. In the northern dialect a plural form of **Шумо** also exists, **Шумоён**. Similarly, the pronoun **мо** is also used for 'I' in this dialect and has the plural form **моён** for 'we.'

2.2 Interrogative pronouns

Interrogative pronouns are used to ask the identity of a noun. The basic interrogative pronouns are **кӣ** 'who?' and **чӣ** 'what?' **Кӣ** is used only for people and **чӣ** for animals and inanimate objects; their plural forms are **киҳо** and **чиҳо**. The word order for interrogative pronouns is the same as in simple sentences; **кӣ** and **чӣ** take the same position in the sentence as the nouns they replace and are not moved to the beginning of the sentence as is done in English.

Карим бо муаллим гап зад, 'Karim chatted <u>with the teacher</u>.'
Карим бо кӣ гап зад? '<u>With whom</u> did Karim chat?'

In addition, **чӣ** can be used adjectivally in front of a noun, in which case it means 'what?': **чӣ китоб** 'what book?' (Note that nouns modified by **чӣ** are not necessarily definite.) A number of other interrogatives are formed from **чӣ** and a general noun (see the list below). Also, **чӣ** is also used just as in English for expressions of wonder and surprise (note the use of the indefinite clitic corresponding to the indefinite article *a/an*): **Чй боге!** 'What a garden!'

Some of the other interrogative pronouns have the same form as interrogative adjectives, and when used adjectivally precede the noun. The following are other important interrogative words (pronouns, adverbs, and adjectives) and phrases in Tajiki.

кай 'when?'
кучо 'where?' (*acts as noun*)
чанд 'how many, how much?'
кадом 'which?'
чаро 'why?'

чй қадар 'how much?'
чй тавр 'how?' (*manner*)
чй хел 'how?' (*condition*)
чандум 'which?' (*of a series*)
чй гуна 'what kind?'

Чаро has the colloquial equivalents **чиба/чида**, and is often replaced by **барои чй** 'for what?'

2.3 Demonstrative pronouns

Demonstrative pronouns are used to point out things or refer to nouns that can be identified from one's surroundings or from the course of the preceding conversation.

The basic demonstrative pronouns are **ин** 'this' and **он** 'that'; they can also be used (unlike in English) to refer to people, and in this use mean 'this/that person,' and thus 'he/she.' (To indicate politeness it is better to say **ин кас** 'this person' and **он кас** 'that person,' which are treated grammatically as plural in the northern dialect to show respect: **Ин кас раисанд**, 'He/she is the company head/our boss,' not the singular **раис аст**.) As in English, **ин** indicates something close to the speaker and **он** something further away. As pronouns they have the plural forms **инхо** 'these' and **онхо** 'those.' They can also be used as demonstrative adjectives, in which case they precede the noun they modify and never take a plural suffix: **ин китоб** 'this book,' **он гурба** 'that cat,' **он китобхо** 'those books,' **ин хонахо** 'these houses.' The demonstrative adjectives always precede numerals: **ин ду сар гӯсфанд** 'these two sheep.'

Ин китоб аст, 'This is a book.'
Ин китоб нав аст, 'This book is new.' (*not 'This is a new book.'*)
Ин китобхо наванд, 'These books are new.'
Инхо наванд, 'These are new.'
but not: **Инхо китобхо наванд.** (*This is not correct.*)

Он тиреза аст, 'That is a window.'
Он тиреза калон аст, 'That window is large.'
(not 'That is a large window.')
Он тирезаҳо калонанд, 'Those windows are large.'
Онҳо калонанд, 'Those are large.'
but not: **Онҳо тирезаҳо калонанд.** (This is not correct.)

When pointing something out or handing something over, Tajiks use the special presentative pronouns **мана** 'this here' and **ана** 'that there.'

Ана, он китоб. 'That book right there; there's the book.'
Мана, ин нома. 'This letter right here; here's the letter.'

Besides their basic use to refer to specific things, **ин** and **он** are used for:

1) *anaphora, or reference to other words in speech*: **Вай инро гуфта рафт...** 'He said this and left...' (as in English, **ин** is used to indicate something about to be said and **он** to indicate something that has already been mentioned); and

2) *to indicate object clauses*: **Сабаби ин он аст, ки ӯ бемор аст**, 'The reason for this is (this), that he is sick.' (See Chapter 5, Section 2.)

Ин and **он** have the emphatic forms **ҳамин** and **ҳамон**, which can be used as pronouns and as adjectives.

ҳамин китоб 'this very book, this same book'
ҳамин одамҳо 'these very people, these same people'
ҳамон шахс 'that very person'
ҳамон духтарҳо 'those very girls, those same girls'
Ҳамонҳо хубанд. 'Only those/just those right there are good.'
Ҳаминҳо пуранд. 'Only these/just these right here are full.'

Also commonly used are the demonstrative pronouns and adjectives (also often used as adverbs) **чунин** 'like this, in this way' and **чунон** 'like that, in that way, thus.' They are often best translated 'such, so.' With this meaning **чунон** is used to form correlative clauses (Chapter 5, Section 5).

2.4 Indefinite pronouns

Indefinite pronouns are those like *everybody, something, anyone,* and *nothing* that pick out all, some, or none of a group; even though they include words like *everybody,* they are called "indefinite" because they do not pick out or point to a particular or specific person, place, or thing, but instead refer to the members of a group or class. Most indefinite pronouns are formed in three series that correspond very roughly to the *some-, no-,* and *every*-series of English; in Tajiki they are formed by adding an appropriate modifier to the nouns **кас** 'person' and **чиз** 'thing.' The *some*-series uses the indefiniteness clitic **-e** (which can be replaced or emphasized with **як** 'one' or **ягон** 'several'); the *no*-series, **хеч** 'no'; and the *every*-series, **ҳар** 'each.' They are formed the same way as indefinite adverbs and adjectives (*somehow, anywhere,* etc.). Because their forms do not match up in a simple fashion with English indefinites and depend on the form of the verb of the sentence, indefinite pronouns and adverbs are discussed together in detail in the chapter on adverbs, Chapter 4, Section 1.5.

Besides those discussed above, the pronouns **ҳама** 'all,' **аксар** 'most/majority' **ҳар** 'each,' **бисёр** 'many,' **зиёд** '(a great) many,' and **баъзе** 'some, a few' are extremely important and very common; as in English, grammatically they are considered plural. All of them may be used as indefinite adjectives as well. A few other indefinite pronouns are fairly common.

фалон 'a certain someone, so-and-so'
фалонӣ 'some person'
(*indefinite, largely equivalent to* **шахсе** *'a person'*)

3. Adjectives and determiners

Adjectives are words that describe, delimit, or pick out (*modify*) nouns, such as *green, tall, beautiful, humane, all, many, which, this,* and *that.* Simple adjectives describe nouns, interrogative adjectives are used to ask which of a group or class of things a noun refers to (*which?*), and demonstrative adjectives (which in a broad sense include indefinite adjectives) point out or narrow down which thing or things in a group or class a noun refers to (*the, this, these, some, all, many, no*). Interrogative and demonstrative adjectives are often classified as part of a distinct class of words in English, *determiners* (which also includes articles, possessive nouns, possessive pronouns, and to some extent numerals used adjectivally in English), because as a group they behave rather differently from simple adjectives (they must occur before any other words in a noun phrase and in general two determiners cannot occur in the same noun phrase, for example).

The grammatical differences between simple adjectives and determiners are even stronger in Tajiki: Determiners always come before the noun they modify, while simple adjectives almost always come after the noun. Because determiners form noun phrases differently than simple adjectives do and are closely tied to definiteness, they are discussed much more fully in section 5.1 below and in Chapter 3, Section 2. However, it is appropriate at this point to list the important demonstrative, interrogative, and indefinite adjectives, many of which are also used as pronouns.

As mentioned above, **ин/он** 'this/that,' **ҳамин/ҳамон** 'this/that very one,' and **чунин/чунон** 'such (a one), (one) like this/that' are the important demonstrative pronouns; all of them are also used as demonstrative adjectives. The following interrogative pronouns are also used as adjectives:

чӣ   'what?'
кадом   'which?'
чанд   'how many, how much?'
чандум   'which?' (*of a series*)

In addition, the following interrogative phrases can modify a noun: **чӣ гуна** 'what kind?' and **чӣ қадар** 'how much, what quantity?'

The important indefinite adjectives include: **ҳама** 'all,' **ҳар** 'each,' **бисёр** 'many,' **зиёд** '(a great) many,' **чанд/чандин** 'some, several,' **якчанд** 'several,' **ягон** 'any, a few,' **баъзе** 'some, a few,' **як** 'one,' and **ҳеҷ** 'no.'

3.1 Comparatives and superlatives

Comparatives (*bigger, greener,* etc.) and superlatives (*biggest, greenest,* etc.) are used to compare one noun with others in the quality of the adjective. Comparatives (showing more of a quality than others in a group) are always formed in Tajiki with the sufix **-тар**, which takes the stress:

сафед 'white,' **сафедтар** 'whiter'
гарм 'hot,' **гармтар** 'hotter'

The basis of comparison (shown by *than* in English) is indicated by the preposition **аз** 'from' or (much less commonly) **то** 'until':

аз барф сафедтар 'whiter than snow'
аз ёқут сурхтар 'redder than ruby'

The phrase *than ever* is expressed with **аз пеш** 'than before': **аз пеш гармтар** 'hotter than ever, hotter than before.' To say *more than ever*, Tajiki uses the phrase **беш аз пеш**.

The superlative (showing the *most* of a quality among a group) is formed in two ways; they do not differ in meaning. First, one can use the comparative and **аз ҳама** 'than all': **аз ҳама сафедтар** 'whitest.' Alternatively, the suffix **-тарин** indicates the superlative:

сафед 'white,' **сафедтарин** 'whitest'
гарм 'hot,' **гармтарин** 'hottest'
сурх 'red,' **сурхтарин** 'reddest'

беҳтарин рӯзҳои зиндагии ман
'the best days of my life'

When modifying a noun, the superlative in **-тарин** is a determiner and thus precedes the noun, while the comparative is a simple adjective and must follow the noun. Almost all adjectives add **-тар** and **-тарин** to the end of the simple adjective, but a few adjectives add **-тар** and **-тарин** to a different stem, just like English *good/better/best* and *bad/worse/worst*:

хуб 'good,' **беҳтар** 'better,' **беҳтарин** 'best'
Note: беҳ *'good' is usually used in Tajiki only as a predicate*

бисёр 'many,' **бештар** 'more,' **бештарин** 'most'
Note: беш *is an adverb meaning 'more'*

In fact, the basic marker of the superlative is the suffix **-ин**; **-тарин** is a compound suffix used commonly with all adjectives whose meanings allow a superlative. The suffix **-ин** is used less frequently, but it can be found in such words as **нахустин** 'first,' **пасин** 'last,' and **беҳин** 'best.'

3.2 Adjectives used as nouns

Adjectives can be used as nouns without adding any suffixes, in which case they have the sense 'the...one':

сурх 'red, the red one' (*but not the name of the color*)
бузург 'high, the high one'
калон 'large, the large one'

3.3 Numerals

The names of the numbers 1-10 in Tajiki are as follows:

як	1	чор (чаҳор)	4	ҳафт	7	даҳ	10
ду	2	панч	5	ҳашт	8		
се	3	шаш	6	нӯҳ	9		

The final consonant in the numerals for 7-10 is not pronounced in normal speech unless a vowel closely follows it. There are two words for 'zero,' **нол** (from Russian) and **сифр** (from Arabic, also the source of the English words *zero* and *cipher*); as in English, they are less commonly used than the other numerals.

As in English, the numbers for the teens and the decades (multiples of ten less than a hundred) in Tajiki have to be learned individually. The numbers for the teens end in **даҳ** '10' preceded by the number for the remainder over ten, in most cases in modified form (particularly involving consonant mutations like those of Russian, as well as some vowel changes):

ёздаҳ	11	шонздаҳ	16
дувоздаҳ	12	ҳабдаҳ	17
сездаҳ	13	ҳаждаҳ	18
чордаҳ	14	нуздаҳ	19
понздаҳ	15		

The numbers for the decades are more irregular:

бист	20	шаст	60
сӣ	30	ҳафтод	70
чил(чиҳил)	40	ҳаштод	80
панҷоҳ	50	навад	90

Numbers for the hundreds and thousands are formed as in English, with the number of hundreds or thousands followed by **сад** '100' or **ҳазор** '1000,' except that unlike in English the hundreds are written as one word: **дусад** '200,' **се ҳазор** '3000.' For larger numbers Tajiki uses **миллион** 'million' and follows the British, German, and Russian system of **миллиард** 'milliard' for a thousand millions and **биллион** 'billion' for a million millions (a billion and a trillion, respectively, in the American and French system).

The other numbers are formed as compounds of these, much as in English; the numbers go from largest to smallest and must be connected with the enclitic **-у** 'and.' (When followed by **-у**, word-final **ҳ** is pronounced.) Since **й** is automatically added between vowels, **-у** becomes **-ю** when added to numbers ending in vowels (thus, **ду**, **се**, and **сӣ**: **дую, сею, сию**; the first two of these generally only occur with fractions). Compound numbers are not written as one word:

бисту ҳафт	27	ҳафтоду як	71
саду чор	104	саду ҳабдаҳ	117
дусаду бист	220		

чорсаду наваду панҷ	495
ҳафт ҳазору сесаду панҷоҳу нӯҳ	7359
бисту панҷ ҳазор	25,000
сесаду ҳафтод ҳазор	370,000

панҷ миллиарду чорсаду наваду ду миллиону шашсаду сию ҳафт ҳазору чорсаду ҳаштоду як	5,492,637,481

The fraction *a/b* is formed regularly by saying the equivalent of "from (**аз**) *b*, *a* parts (**ҳисса**)." Thus, *two-thirds* is **аз се ду ҳисса** and *three-fifths* is **аз панҷ се ҳисса**. The construction with **тақсим** 'division' (**ду тақсими се** 'two divided by three,' **се тақсими панҷ** 'three divided by five') is more formal and largely restricted to mathematical contexts. In addition, there are several special fractional terms. *One-half* is **ним**; terms for unitary fractions (fractions with one in the numerator) from *one-third* on are formed by suffixing **як** to the numeral for the denominator: **сеяк** 'a third,' **чоряк** 'a fourth, a quarter.' Also, there are several Arabic words for fractions that are falling increasingly out of use in the spoken language: **нисф** 'half,' **сулс** 'third,' and **рубъ** 'quarter.' Fractions follow whole numbers in the normal fashion:

дую ним	2 ½	**яку сеяк**	1 1/3
панчу сеяк	5 1/3	**бисту хафту аз панч се хисса**	27 3/5

Fractions of a whole (*half of the pie, a tenth of your income*) are indicated by possessive izofat (see Section 5.2 below): **ними палав** 'half of the pilaf,' **сеяки себ** 'a third of the apples,' **нисфи шахр** 'half of the city,' **аз панч се хиссаи одамон** 'three-fifths of the people.'

A numeral often follows **хар** 'each, all': **хар ду** 'both,' **хар чор** 'all four.' **Хар як** 'each and every one' emphasizes every member of a group and thus gives no information about the size of the group. On the other hand, if the number is two or more, this construction emphasizes the number and serves to focus on each member of the group rather than the group itself. Although this is not always true, much of the time a phrase like **хар ду** 'both' implies that each member of the group is pursuing his or her own activity or is being acted on individually rather than as a group: **Хар ду мард кор карда истода буданд**, 'Both men were working (usually: on their own jobs).' If necessary, the fact that they were working together is conveyed by **якчоя** 'together' or a similar word, in which case the use of **хар** emphasizes that both men were working on the job, not just that there were two men working.

To indicate an approximate number, it is common to say two successive numerals:

ду-се 'two or three,' **се-чор** 'three or four,' **панч-шаш** 'five or six'

To indicate that people or things are acting or being treated in groups of the same size, one merely says the numeral twice: **як-як** 'one by one,' **ду-ду** 'in pairs, by pairs,' **се-се** 'in threes, by threes,' etc. The same can be done with nouns indicating groups: **даста** 'bunch, group,' **даста-даста** 'in groups'; **фавч** 'troop, host,' **фавч-фавч** 'troop after troop, in a throng.'

3.4 Adjectives with measures

Adjectives and adverbs are frequently used with measures of distance, direction, time, and other quantities in English and Tajiki, for example *40 feet long*, *two miles north*, and *20 inches tall*. In Tajiki the measure is placed immediately before the adjective or adverb; in certain cases (temperature, for example) Tajiki requires an adjective or adverb where English does not:

чил дараҷа гарм '40 degrees Celsius (lit., 40 degrees hot)'
ду метр баланд 'two meters tall'
се километр дур 'three kilometers away (distant)'

Measures are frequently used with comparatives:

чор дараҷа гармтар 'four degrees (Celsius) hotter'
ду метр баландтар 'two meters taller'

Thus, we have the following (note that there is no distinct word in Tajiki for *too* meaning 'in excess'; this sense is conveyed by context):

камтар аз 100 сомонӣ 'less than 100 somoni'
100 сомонӣ кам '100 somoni too little'
100 сомонӣ камтар '100 somoni less'

To indicate frequency or rate, there are two constructions, one with possessive izofat and the other with a prepositional phrase; frequency is indicated with **бор/маротиба** 'time, occasion':

соле ду бор/(дар) як сол ду бор 'twice a year'
соате ҳашт доллар/(дар) як соат ҳашт доллар '$8 an hour'

3.5 Ordinal numerals

Ordinal numerals are used to indicate position in a series, like *first*, *third*, and *seventy-fifth*. The ordinal numerals are usually formed with the suffix **-ум** (**-юм** after a vowel):

якум 'first,' **дуюм** 'second,' **сеюм** 'third,' **чорум** 'fourth'

There are two other words for *first*, **аввал** (an Arabic loanword) and **нахустин** (a determiner).

In addition, there is a second form of the ordinal suffix, **-умин/юмин**. Ordinal numerals in **-ум** are simple adjectives (and follow the noun), while those in **-умин** are determiners (and thus precede the noun). There is a slight difference in meaning between the two forms: **-умин** tends to indicate a set ordering and is in general more emphatic than **-ум**.

In literary Tajiki there are alternate forms for *second*, *third*, and *thirtieth*, **дуввум(ин)**, **севвум(ин)**, and **сиввум(ин)**. The special form **аввал** 'first' has the determiner form **аввалин**.

4. Compound and derived nominals

To this point we have not distinguished simple nominals, which contain only one meaningful part, from those that are formed from smaller units. Compound nouns and adjectives are those that contain two or more independent words, like *bookshop*, *loveblind*, and *underdog*, while derived nouns and adjectives are formed from independent words with prefixes and suffixes (that is, elements that cannot occur by themselves as independent words). In English there is often disagreement whether a compound word should be written as one word, as two separate words, or with a hyphen; there is much less uncertainty in Tajiki.

4.1. Compound nouns and adjectives

There are three basic types of compound nominals, differing in how the nominals are connected.

a. Quite often the elements of a compound nominal are joined directly:

мӯй 'hair' + **сафед** 'white' = **мӯйсафед** 'old man'
ҳам 'same' + **соя** 'shadow' = **ҳамсоя** 'neighbor'

This is quite common with adjectives formed from participial phrases:

аз 'from' + **даст** 'hand' + **рафта** 'gone'
= **аздастрафта** 'lost'

b. Often two nominals are joined with the conjunction **у** 'and'; the resulting phrase is treated as an indivisible unit and written as one word:

син(н) 'age' + **у** 'and' + **сол** 'year' = **синнусол** 'age'
(remember that the second **н** in **син(н)** is not pronounced or written word-finally, but does appear when a suffix is added)

c. Finally, another vowel might be added between the two nouns to break up consonant clusters:

пир 'old' + **а** + **зан** 'woman' = **пиразан** 'old woman'

An important group of nouns is formed this way with the past and present stems of verbs:

гуфт 'spoke' + **у** + **гӯй** 'speaking' = **гуфтугӯй** 'telling'
дав 'running' + **о** + **дав** 'running' = **даводав** 'fuss, bustle'
рафт 'gone' + **у** + **о** 'coming' = **рафтуо** 'visiting'
чуст 'searched' + **у** + **чӯй** 'searching' = **чустучӯй** 'searching'

4.2 Derived nominals

There is a wide variety of prefixes and suffixes used to form new nouns and adjectives. Common ways of deriving nouns and adjectives from verbs are discussed in Chapter 3, Sections 5.1.f and g. The most important ways of deriving nouns and adjectives from each other are:

a. The suffix -й. This suffix is used to form adjectives from nouns and abstract nouns from adjectives. It is very commonly used to convert a noun to an adjective in cases where English would simply join two nouns, such as "wood door" or "copper plate"; unlike English, Tajiki distinguishes very carefully between nouns and adjectives and usually requires an adjective (like "wooden" or "coppery") where English would use a noun. When -й is used to form an adjective, it can have one of a number of meanings, such as indicating the material out of which something is made, nationality, the character of weather, or more generally something associated with or intended for the noun:

чӯб 'wood'   **чӯбӣ** 'wooden'
Амрико 'America'   **амрикойӣ** 'American'
борон 'rain'   **боронӣ** 'rainy'

When used to make a noun, **-ӣ** indicates the abstract quality of the adjective:

шиносо 'acquainted' **шиносоӣ** 'acquaintance'

The suffix takes the form **-гӣ** after the vowel **a**:

хона 'home' **хонагӣ** 'of/for the home'
(*as in* **вазифаи хонагӣ** 'homework')

b. The suffix -истон. This suffix is added to a noun to indicate a place abundant in that noun. While it is best-known for forming country names from ethnic names, it is used more widely. For example, from **гул** 'flower, rose' is formed **гулистон** 'place of flowers' (the name of a village in Azerbaijan where a famous treaty with Russia was signed in 1813), as well as 'The Rose Garden' (a famous book by Saadi). Similarly,

бемор 'ill' **бемористон** 'hospital'
себ 'apple' **Себистон** 'place of apples' (*a village in Tajikistan*)

c. The suffix -a. This suffix forms nouns or adjectives from other nouns and adjectives; the resulting word has a meaning related in some way to that of the original word: **банд** 'busy, bound,' **банда** 'slave.' Its most important uses are these:

> 1. When suffixed to numbers, **-a** gives a noun that contains that number of parts or divisions or is otherwise closely related to that number: **панҷ** 'five,' **панҷа**, 'the five fingers, hand, paw'; **ҳафт** 'seven,' **ҳафта** 'week.'
> 2. When suffixed to a measure **of** time, **-a** gives an **adjective** meaning "having the age of..." or "lasting as long as...":
> **ду сол** 'two years,' **дусола** 'two-year-old'; **се моҳ** 'three months,' **семоҳа** 'three months old, lasting three months.'
> 3. A similar construction is used with nouns modified by a numeral to name something with that number of parts: **ду чарх** 'two wheels,' **дучарха** 'bicycle.'

These adjectives are always written as one word and not hyphenated as they sometimes are in English. These adjectives are common with **рӯз** 'day,' **моҳ** 'month,' and **сол** 'year.' Note that one can then add the suffix **-ӣ** (which, because it follows **а**, becomes **-гӣ**) to form a noun naming the condition of having that age or lasting that length of time:

Вай аз дусолагӣ хонда метавонист,
'From the age of two he was able to read.'

However, **-а** cannot be added to a word that already ends in it; instead one adds the suffix **-ина**: **ҳафта** 'week' > **ҳафтаина** 'weekly.'

d. The suffix -она. The suffix **-она** is used with time words to indicate that the action or condition either occurs regularly at that time, lasts during that time, or is associated with that time:

рӯзона 'during the day, daily'
шабона 'during the night, nightly'
солона 'yearly'

It is used more generally to indicate something particularly characteristic of or intended for a noun:

мардона 'men's, for men'
занона 'women's, for women'
сагона 'of dogs; irascible'
ғарбиёна 'western, occidental'
ваҳшиёна 'vicious, inhuman'

e. The suffix -гар. The **-гар** suffix is used to name the creator in a broad sense of the root noun: **кимиё** 'chemistry,' **кимиёгар** 'chemist'; **варзиш** 'sports,' **варзишгар** 'sportsman.'

f. The suffix -зор. The suffix **-зор** is used to form a noun naming a place abundant in the base noun, usually a type of park or garden: **дарахт** 'tree,' **дарахтзор** 'arbor, orchard'; **ток** 'grapevine,' **токзор** 'vineyard'; **лола** 'tulip,' **лолазор** 'tulip garden'; **себ** 'apple,' **себзор** 'apple orchard.'

g. The suffix -чӣ. The agentive suffix **-чӣ** is used to form the names of professions from nouns associated with the profession. Thus, from **иқтисод** 'economy' is formed **иқтисодчӣ** 'economist,' and from **телефон** 'telephone' is formed **телефончӣ** '(telephone) operator.'

h. The suffix -ча. The diminutive suffix **-ча** is added to nouns, especially animates, to indicate something young or small: **гурба** 'cat,' **гурбача** 'kitten'; **моҳӣ** 'fish,' **моҳича** 'small fish, fry'; **курсӣ** 'chair,' **курсича** 'stool'; **халта** 'sack,' **халтача** 'tote bag.'

i. The suffix -ак. The suffix **-ак** is used (1) like **-ча** to form diminutive nouns, and (2) nouns associated with, resembling, or metaphorically comparable to another noun. Thus, from **чанг** 'claw' is formed **чангак** 'fork,' and from **гӯш** 'ear' is formed **гӯшак** 'telephone receiver.' Similarly, from **шаб** 'evening' and **паридан/пар** 'to fly' is formed **шабпарак** 'butterfly.'

j. The suffix -гоҳ. The suffix **-гоҳ** 'place' is used to form the names of places characterized by or devoted to the root noun: **дониш** 'knowledge,' **донишгоҳ** 'university'; **фуруд** 'dismount,' **фурудгоҳ** 'airport.'

k. Adjectival derivational affixes. There are many prefixes and suffixes that serve to form adjectives from nouns. The most common prefixes include the following:

Prefix	Root	New adjective
бо-	ақл 'reason, intellect' адаб 'politeness' истеъдод 'talent, ability' маърифат 'education' тантана 'festivities'	боақл 'wise' боадаб 'polite' боистеъдод 'talented' бомаърифат 'intelligent' ботантана 'festive'
бе-	ақл 'reason, intellect' шарм 'modesty, shame' гуноҳ 'sin' савод 'literacy' шубҳа 'doubt'	беақл 'foolish' бешарм 'shameless' бегуноҳ 'sinless' бесавод 'illiterate' бешубҳа 'undoubted(ly)'
но-	дон 'knowing' тарс 'fear' дуруст 'correct' қулай 'comfortable' пурра 'complete'	нодон 'stupid' нотарс 'fearless' нодуруст 'incorrect' ноқулай 'uncomfortable' нопурра 'incomplete'

The following suffixes are most commonly used to form adjectives from nouns:

Prefix	Root	New adjective
-ин	санг 'stone (*n.*)' чӯб 'wood' хишт 'brick (*n.*)' ранг 'color'	сангин 'stone (*adj.*)' чӯбин 'wooden' хиштин 'brick (*adj.*)' рангин 'colored'
-гин	хашм 'fury, anger' ғам 'grief, sorrow'	хашмгин 'angry, furious' ғамгин 'sorrowful, sad'
-нок	нам 'moisture' дард 'pain' бӯй 'smell'	намнок 'humid' дарднок 'painful' бӯйнок 'smelly, stinking'
-манд	дониш 'knowledge' ҳунар 'skill, talent' сарват 'wealth'	донишманд 'wise, learned' ҳунарманд 'skillful, clever' сарватманд 'rich'

5. Noun phrases

Noun phrases are formed in English by adding determiners and simple adjectives in front of the noun they modify in fairly strict order (thus, determiners precede simple adjectives, and among simple adjectives, adjectives of size precede adjectives of color, which precede adjectives of material: *these big green steel cans*), except in very literary or poetic language: *My car, a big house, our four well-fed cats, those three cars of his* (but *a midnight dark and dreary*). As previously mentioned, in Tajiki determiners must precede the noun, while simple adjectives and possessors must follow the noun, which takes a special suffix (*izofat*) indicating the noun is modified.

5.1 Determiners

Tajiki determiners include interrogative adjectives, demonstrative adjectives, numerals, the superlative form of simple adjectives, and the preposed form of ordinal numbers. In most cases determiners are automatically formally definite, but there are some important exceptions.

First, the following are always indefinite: **ҳеҷ** 'no,' **як** 'one,' **ягон** 'some, a few,' and **чанд** 'several' (whereas **якчанд** 'several' and **чандин** 'some, several' are definite).

Second, the following determiners are either definite or indefinite depending on context: **бисёр** 'many' and **чӣ** 'what?'

5.2 Izofat

Izofat is an enclitic **и** used to indicate that a noun (or occasionally another nominal) is modified by another noun, an adjective, or a pronoun. The most common uses of izofat are to indicate attribution, in which an adjective or adjective phrase follows the noun: **шаҳри зебо** 'a beautiful city,' **ноҳияи дур** 'a distant region,' **иқлими гарм** 'warm climate'; and possession, in which case the noun is followed by a pronoun or another noun: **шаҳри ман** 'my city,' **ноҳияи Ҳисор** 'the region of Hisor,' **иқлими Тоҷикистон** 'the climate of Tajikistan.'

Note that the adjective always modifies the noun immediately before it, so it must come before any noun or pronoun that possesses the noun it modifies; in that case the adjective takes izofat:

хонаи *зебои зан*	'the <u>beautiful</u> house of the *woman*'
хонаи *зани зебо*	'the house of the <u>beautiful</u> *woman*'

Adverbs always precede adjectives that they modify, and thus fall between a noun and an adjective in an izofat phrase.

хонаи *хеле зебои зан*	'the *woman's* <u>very beautiful</u> house'
хонаи *зани хеле зебо*	'the <u>very beautiful</u> *woman's* house'

There is no English equivalent to attributive izofat; note that the order of the adjective and noun is opposite that in English. In possessive izofat the possessor follows the noun with izofat (the possessed noun), and possessive izofat can be translated "of."

ҷузвдони Сафина	'the bag of Safina'
модари Парвиз	'the mother of Parviz'

When several nouns are modified by a single adjective (*a red pen and pencil*, for example), they are joined together by **-у** or **ва** 'and' and the izofat comes after the last noun of the series: **хомаю қалами сурх**, 'a red pen and pencil.' This can be ambiguous in Tajiki as in English; **хомаю қалами сурх** can mean either *a red pen and a red pencil* or *a pen and a red pencil*.

When a noun is modified by more than one adjective, the adjectives can be joined together with **-у** or **ва** 'and' or by izofat: **хонаи калону нав** and **хонаи калони нав** both mean 'a big new house.' The order of adjectives does not matter in Tajiki; both **хонаи нави калон** and **хонаи калони нав** are acceptable in Tajiki, whereas 'a new big house' is not usually an acceptable word order in English.

Pronouns act just the same as nouns in possessive izofat: **китоби ман** 'my book,' **мошини вайҳо** 'their car.' This is true of the interrogative pronouns **кӣ** and **чӣ** as much as the personal pronouns: **китоби кӣ?** 'whose book?'; **китоби чӣ?** 'what (kind of) book?' (answered by, for example, **китоби таърих** 'a book of history'). Note that if **ин** and **он** are used in this way with izofat they must be pronouns, so that **китоби ин** means 'the book of this one, this person's book.' Since the pronoun in possessive izofat acts just like a possessive noun, it comes last in the izofat phrase: **хонаи нави мо**, 'our new house.' A possessive izofat phrase with a personal pronoun is treated grammatically as always definite; the indefinite sense of 'a friend of mine' is shown with **як** 'one' or **чанд** 'some, several': **як дӯсти ман** 'a friend of mine,' **яке аз дӯстҳои ман** 'one of my friends,' **чанд дӯсти ман** 'some friends of mine.' Such indefinite phrases are still treated grammatically as definite and as direct objects require **-ро**:

> **Падарам як дӯсти туро диданд,**
> 'My father saw a friend of yours.'

In the literary language, if **ман** in a possessive izofat phrase is followed by **-ро**, it loses the final **н**:

> **Падарам яке аз дӯстҳои маро диданд,**
> 'My father saw one of my friends.'

However, in colloquial Tajiki the definite direct object marker is **-(р)а**, which in the *northern* dialect does not cause the final **н** to drop out. Thus, the combination is pronounced **мана** and **мара** in the northern and southern dialects of Tajiki, respectively (note that in the southern dialect the subject is not usually treated as plural to show respect):

> **Падарам яке аз дӯстҳои мана диданд,**
> 'My father saw one of my friends.' (N)
> **Падарам яке аз дӯстҳои мара дид,**
> 'My father saw one of my friends.' (S)

Other uses of izofat are:

a. to relate a personal and family name:

Мирзои Салимпур	'Mirzoi Salimpur'
Ҳумоюни Шаҳриёр	'Humoyuni Shahriyor'
Парвизи Ромишгар	'Parvizi Romishgar'
Сафинаи Акрамдухт	'Safinai Akramdukht'

b. to relate a nonprofessional title and a Tajik name or position:

| ҷаноби Шаҳриёр | 'Mister Shahriyor' |
| ҷаноби раис | 'Mister Chief' |

c. to relate the possessive and attributive members of a compound izofat phrase:

духтари зебои ҳамсояи ман
'my neighbor's beautiful daughter'
қалами нави кӯдаки танбал
'the new pencil of a lazy child'

d. to relate a place name and its geographical category:

шаҳри Душанбе	'Dushanbe city'
кӯҳи Помир	'Mount Pamir'
уқёнуси Атлас	'the Atlantic Ocean'
дарёи Вахш	'the Vakhsh River'

Tajiki pronouns can also be modified by an adjective with izofat; the meaning is very similar to English phrases like *poor me* and *lucky you*: **мани бечора** 'poor me.'

A numeral can take izofat with a plural personal pronoun or the corresponding personal possessive marker (see the next section) to indicate the number of people referred to; thus, **дуи мо / дуямон** means 'we two, (the) two of us.'

5.3 Personal possessive markers

Besides izofat followed by a personal pronoun, Tajiki has another way of indicating possession, the personal possessive markers. These suffixes indicate the person and number of the possessor, and effectively replace the izofat and pronoun:

-ам = -и ман 'my' -амон = -и мо 'our'
-ат = -и ту 'your (sg)' -атон = -и шумо 'your (pl)'
-аш = -и вай 'his, her, its' -ашон = -и онҳо 'their'

Номи Шумо чист? / Номатон чист? 'What is <u>your</u> name?'
Номи ман Лола аст / Номам Лола аст, '<u>My</u> name is Lola.'
Номи вай чист? / Номаш чист? 'What is <u>his</u> name?'
Номи вай Бежан аст / Номаш Бежан аст, '<u>His</u> name is Bezhan.'

If the noun is modified by adjectives, the personal possessive marker is attached to the last adjective in the phrase: **хонаи нави калонамон** 'our big new house.' A noun or noun phrase with a personal possessive marker is always treated grammatically as definite, and thus as a direct object must take **-ро**.

Шумо хонаи нави калонамонро дидед?
'Did you see our big new house?'

Such phrases can be made indefinite in meaning with **як** 'one' or **чанд** 'some, several,' as can possessive izofat phrases with personal pronouns; grammatically, however, they are treated as definite.

Падарам як дӯстатро диданд,
'Father saw a friend of yours.'

Because **-ро** is reduced in colloquial Tajiki following consonants to **-а**, the personal possessive markers of direct objects have the colloquial forms **-ама, -ата, -аша**, etc.

In colloquial Tajiki it is common to use the 3rd person personal possessive markers to indicate which members one means of a group that is actually on hand; most commonly either an adjective or a demonstrative pronoun is modified by the personal possessive marker. In this usage **-аш** is used with singular pronouns and adjectives. With plural pronouns **-ашон** is optional, but it must be used with adjectives; if the adjective takes **-ҳо** as well, this adds a slight touch of indefiniteness. They are best translated 'the...one(s)':

инаш 'this one' инҳо(ашон) 'these here'
сафедаш 'the white one' сафед(ҳо)ашон 'the white ones'

Инаша тед, 'Give me this one here.'
Сафедашона гирам, 'I'll take (let me get) the white ones.'
Сафедҳояшона гирам, 'I'll take (some of the) white ones.'

5.4 Reflexive, reciprocal, and intensive pronouns.

Reflexive pronouns are used to refer back to the subject, that is, to indicate that the subject is acting on or for itself. In English the reflexive pronouns are *myself, yourself, himself,* etc. Tajiki reflexive pronouns are formed very much the same way, by adding the appropriate personal possessive marker to **худ** 'self':

худам 'myself' **худамон** 'ourselves'
худат 'yourself' **худатон** 'yourselves'
худаш 'him-, her-, itself' **худашон** 'themselves'

Alternatively, it is common to use the izofat and personal pronoun (**худи ман, худи вай,** etc.); this is most common if the reflexive pronoun were to be immediately followed by the predicate marker in an equational sentence, and frequently occurs in poetry and songs to fit the meter.

The reflexive pronouns can be used as direct objects (and being definite must take **-ро**) or as the objects of prepositions.

Ман худамро нағз ҳис кардам,
'I felt good.' (**ҳис кардан,** 'to feel')
Онҳо худашонро дар ойина диданд,
'They saw themselves in the mirror.'

Reciprocal pronouns are used to indicate that the people named by the subject (which must be plural) are acting on or for *each other*. In English the reciprocal pronouns are *each other* and *one another*. The reflexive pronouns in Tajiki are **якдигар** and **ҳамдигар**.

Онҳо якдигарро дар ойина диданд,
'They saw each other in the mirror.'

In English the reflexive pronoun is also used for emphasis, in which case it is called an intensive pronoun: *I did it myself*, *They themselves are the crazy ones*, etc. The reflexive pronouns are used the same way in Tajiki; they follow the words in the sentence that are being emphasized (a connotation English can convey in the same way, but usually in other ways).

Ман худам дидам, 'I saw it myself.'
Ман худам онро кардам, '*I myself* did it, I did it *myself.*'
(Emphasizes that I was the one to do it, as opposed to someone else)

Ман онро худам кардам, 'I myself did *that*, *That* I did (myself).'
(Emphasizes that that is what I did myself, as opposed to what other people had a hand in)

It is common to omit the subject when it is followed by the intensive pronoun. The intensive pronoun occurs by itself in commands.

Худаш гуфт, 'He said it himself.'
Худатон нависед, 'Write it yourself!'

6. Prepositions and prepositional phrases

Prepositions are words indicating relationships of various sorts between nouns or between a noun and a verb, like *from, to, above, below, beside,* and *about*; in English and Tajiki a preposition is followed by a noun, noun phrase, or pronoun (which is called the object of the preposition) to form a prepositional phrase, such as *above the clouds, in the dumps, over the rainbow, about Bill,* and *beside me*. However, not all English prepositions are translated with prepositions in Tajiki; the important exceptions will be given below. Note that in colloquial English it is possible under certain circumstances to separate an object from its preposition and move it to the beginning of a clause or sentence: <u>What</u> did you want to talk to me <u>about</u>? is much more common and natural in colloquial American English than <u>About what</u> did you want to talk to me? In Tajiki, however, it is unacceptable to move the object of a preposition to the beginning of a sentence; prepositions must always be immediately followed by their objects.

6.1 Classes of prepositions

There are three classes of prepositions in Tajiki.
a. Simple prepositions must be followed by a noun or noun phrase; they are used for the most basic spatial and temporal relationships. There are ten simple prepositions in spoken Tajiki:

аз 'from'	**дар** 'at, in'	**бо** 'with'
бе 'without'	**то** 'until'	**ба** 'towards'
бар 'over'	**чуз** 'except'	**ғайри** 'except'
барои 'for'		

аз кай 'since when'   **дар хона** 'at home'
бо дӯстам 'with my friend' **бе гурба** 'without a cat'
то кай 'until when'   **ба хонаи Парвиз** 'to Parviz's house'
бар сарам 'over my head'   **чуз ман** 'except me'
ғайри ӯ 'besides him'   **барои падарам** 'for my father'

There are also some combinations of simple prepositions (compound simple prepositions) like: **то ба** 'until,' **ба чуз** 'except for.' The simple prepositions are discussed in much greater detail in the next section.

b. Simple nominal prepositions are nouns which can be used in izofat constructions with other nouns to name relative locations in space and time: **баъди пешин** 'after noon,' **назди модарам** 'near Mother,' **наздики донишгоҳ** 'near the university.' Often they can be used with simple prepositions as well:

Ман баъд аз Дилбар меравам, 'I will go after Dilbar.'
Ман пеш аз Шумо омадам, 'I came before you.'

Typically they are also used alone as conjunctions, adverbs, or adjectives: **баъд** 'later,' **пеш** 'before, earlier,' **наздик** 'close':

Ман баъд меравам, 'I will go later.'
Ман пеш омадам, 'I came before.'
Хонаи ӯ наздик аст, 'His house is close.'

The possessive markers can also be used with compound prepositions and **барои**: **дар миёнамон** 'between us,' **аз болояш** 'from its top,' **бароят** 'for you.' When the 3rd person singular -**аш** is used with prepositions, it is often best translated *the*: **дар миёнаш** 'in the middle,' **аз болояш** 'from the top.'

c. Compound nominal prepositions consist of a simple preposition followed by a simple nominal preposition and are used to indicate more specific spatial and temporal relations than the simple prepositions show. Thus, the basic spatial meaning of **аз** is motion away from; it can be combined with such nominal prepositions as **тараф** 'side,' **байн** 'middle; between,' and **поён** 'feet; bottom' to indicate motion away from the object starting at the location named: **аз тарафи ман** 'from my side,' **аз байни деҳа** 'from the middle of the village,' and **аз поёни шаҳр** 'from the bottom of the city.' Similarly, compound prepositions in **дар** indicate the location where an object is located or an action takes place, and those in **ба** the location towards which motion is directed.

The most important nouns of location used in compound prepositions are the following, with their corresponding equivalent basic English prepositions given:

атроф 'around'	**паҳлӯ** 'side, beside'
байн 'between'	**пеш** 'front'
берун 'outside'	**поён** 'under, below, at the base of'
боло 'over, above'	**пушт** 'behind'
дарун 'inside'	**рӯбарӯй** 'opposite, facing'
зер 'under, below'	**рӯй** 'on top of'
қафо 'behind'	**сӯй** 'side, way'
лаб 'right next to'	**таг** 'under, below'
миён 'among'	**тараф** 'side, beside'
назд 'near'	**тарафи/дасти рост** 'right (side) of'
пас 'behind'	**тарафи/дасти чап** 'left (side) of'

Note: *Many of these nouns have concrete meanings as well; for example,* **лаб** *means 'lip,'* **рӯй** *'face,'* **рӯбарӯй** *'face to face,'* **поён** *'feet,' and* **даст** *'hand.'*

Some English prepositions correspond to a compound nominal preposition containing only one of the three prepositions **аз**, **ба**, and **дар**:

аз миёни/аз байни 'through' (*also expressed with* **аз**)
аз роҳи/аз тариқи 'via'

дар бораи 'about (*concerning*)'
дар баробари 'versus'
дар рафти 'during, in the course of'
ба мисли 'like'
ба муқобили/бар зидди 'against'

Structurally, compound nominal prepositions are simple prepositions followed by noun phrases, so unlike English they are used systematically with interrogative pronouns. Thus, one must say **дар кучо** 'where, where at,' parallel with **аз кучо** 'from where, whence' and **ба кучо** '(to) where, whither'; a simple **кучо** is incorrect. Similarly, one must say **дар ин чо** 'here' and **дар он чо** 'there.' Note that in English *here, there*, and *where* are ambiguous, since they can indicate either location or motion towards; this can cause trouble in Tajiki for English speakers.

A number of English prepositions correspond to other constructions in Tajiki:

новобаста аз 'despite'
оид ба/рочеъ ба 'about (*concerning*)'
(**оид ба** *is more literary than* **дар бораи** *above;*
рочеъ ба *is much more common in Iran*)
доир ба 'according to'
монанд ба 'like' (= **ба мисли, барин** 'like' *above*)
бидуни 'without' (*fairly archaic*)
хангоми/зимни 'during' (*since they are time expressions, they do not need a simple preposition;* **зимни** *is quite formal*)

In addition, many verbs and adjectives require particular prepositions to complete their meaning. While some of these are discussed below, in many cases the choice of preposition is idiomatic and should be learned as part of the adjective or verb:

бой аз 'rich in'
ба...дохил шудан 'to enter/be enrolled in'
ба...ширкат кардан 'to participate in'

In many cases, however, the preposition is what you would expect from English: **бо ...... машғул** 'busy with ......'

6.2 Simple prepositions

The meanings and uses of the Tajiki simple prepositions are as follows.

a. The preposition дар. Дар indicates location; its basic English equivalent is 'at' or 'in.' In speaking it is frequently reduced to да. Its most important uses are as follows:

1) To indicate the place where an action occurs or a condition holds:
Дар Блумингтон тез-тез борон меборад,
'It often rains in Bloomington.'
Мо дар боғ сайругашт кардем,
'We strolled in the park.'

2) To indicate the time at which something occurred:
Дар кӯдакиям ман сабзиро дӯст намедоштам,
'As a child (in childhood) I didn't like carrots.'
Ҳаво дар тобистон хеле гарм аст,
'It's very hot in the summer.'

3) To indicate the respect in which a quality or attribute holds true:
Ӯ дар дониш аз ҳама беҳтар аст,
'She's the best one (lit., better than all) in intelligence.'
Дар пухтупаз касе ба ӯ баробар шуда наметавонад,
'In cooking no one can compete with her.'

In colloquial speech, **дар кучо** is often reduced to **да гучо**, and frequently it is replaced by **канӣ** 'where (at)?'

b. The preposition аз. Аз indicates, most fundamentally, a source; its most basic spatial meaning is separation or motion away from or out of. It is also used to indicate the time from which something starts. In many cases **аз** is used where English would use other prepositions than "out of" or "from"; these must be learned individually as you come across them, but keeping the notion of "source" in mind should help you make sense of them. For example, in English you say that you are worried *about* something, while Tajiks view that something as the source of your worry and thus use **аз**: **Ман**

аз **модарам хавотирам**, 'I am worried *about* my mother.' The most important of its wide variety of uses are the following:

1) To indicate an area, object, or time from which something starts:
   аз кӯдакӣ 'from childhood'
   аз кӯҳ 'from the mountain'   **аз боло** 'from the top'

2) With adjectives like **дур** 'far,' to indicate separation from something:
   Тоҷикистон аз Канада дур аст,
   'Tajikistan is far from Canada.'

3) With verbs like **харидан** 'to buy,' **ёфтан** 'to find,' and **гирифтан** 'to take, obtain, get,' to indicate the source:
   Ҷамшед китобро аз муаллимаш гирифт,
   'Jamshed got the book from his teacher.'
   Ман аз бозор себ харидам,
   'I bought apples from the bazaar.'

4) To indicate motion through or across something:
   Ҳаким аз дарё гузашт, 'Hakim crossed the river.'
   Аз is used in this sense to indicate the extent to which something rises or passes:
   Об аз зонуяш гузашт, 'The water came up to his knees.'
   Вақт аз нимашаб гузашт, 'The time was passing midnight.'
   This use is particularly counterintuitive for English speakers.

5) With comparative adjectives, **аз** means 'than' (**то** may be used instead):
   аз гул нозуктар 'softer than a flower'
   аз тилло қиматтар 'more expensive than gold'

6) To indicate possession. **Аз** can be used in this meaning only with inanimate nouns:
   Ин китоб аз ман аст, 'This book is mine.'
   Ин китоб аз они ман аст, 'This book is mine.'
   Note: аз они *is pronounced* **ини**.

7) To indicate the material out of which something is made:
   аз чӯб 'out of wood'

аз нуқра 'out of silver'
Ин дар аз чӯби тут сохта шудааст,
'This door is made out of mulberry wood.'
Ин гӯшвор аз нуқра сохта шудааст,
'These earrings are made of silver.'

8) To indicate membership in a category or class:
Аз хӯрданиҳо нону қанд ҳаст,
'Of foods, there are bread and **sweets**.'

9) To indicate the cause of or **reason** for an action or condition:
Аз гиря хаста шуд, 'He was (became) tired from crying.'
Аз саросемагӣ пулашро гум кард,
'He lost his money through confusion.'
аз карда пушаймон шудан,
'to be sorry for what one has **done**'

10) With пурсидан 'to ask,' to indicate the person asked:
Ман аз Дилбар саломатии падарашро пурсидам,
'I asked Dilbar about her father's health.'

In Tajiki-Persian poetry **аз** can appear as **зи**:
Зи ишқи Ватан ҷӯш дорад дилам,
'From (for) the love of the Motherland my heart is aboil.'
Зи кӯйи ёр меояд насими боди наврӯзӣ,
'From my sweetheart's house comes the feeling
of the Navruz wind.'

In colloquial Tajiki **аз** is often reduced to **а** in the north and **ай** in the south; **аз куҷо** is often pronounced **а гуҷо** in the north and **ай гуҷо** in the south.

c. The prepositions бо and бе. The prepositions **бо** and **бе** mean "with" and "without," respectively. In English, "with" can indicate accompaniment (*I went with John*) or instrument or means (*I fixed it with duct tape*); **бо** has both meanings as well. Similarly, **бо** is used to indicate the language spoken: **бо забони тоҷикӣ** 'in Tajiki.'

Мо бо Дилбар гап задем, 'We chatted with Dilbar.'

Онҳо бо якдигар чанг карданд, 'They fought with each other.'
Ман номаро бо кордча кушодам,
'I opened the letter with a knife.'
Онҳо бе ман рафтанд, 'They went without me.'

They are also used as prefixes to form adjectives from nouns, in which **бо** indicates the presence of the noun or of a quality associated with it and **бе** its absence.

ақл 'knowledge'	**боақл** 'smart, clever'
дил 'heart'	**бедил** 'heartless, ruthless; cowardly'
мазза 'taste'	**бомазза** 'delicious'
	бемазза 'bland, tasteless'

It is common, both in speaking and in writing, for Tajiks to use **ба** 'towards' in place of **бо**. Thus, instead of **боақл** Tajiks often say **баақл** 'smart,' and you will often hear **ба забони тоҷикӣ** in place of **бо забони тоҷикӣ** 'in Tajiki.' While you should be able to understand this usage when you encounter it, it is considered substandard and should be avoided in your own speech.

d. The prepositions ба and барои. The basic meaning of the preposition **ба** is "direction towards," corresponding to *to, towards, into,* and so on. (**Ба** followed by a personal pronoun often has the meaning 'towards the house of': **ба (хонаи) мо** 'to our house.') It is also used to indicate the indirect object of a sentence—the person to whom the action is directed or who receives the direct object. Usually the indirect object is indicated in English by the preposition *to: I gave the book to him, I read the book to her, I told the story to them.* Note that in all these sentences, the prepositional phrase for the indirect object can be replaced by an object pronoun between the verb and the direct object: *I gave him the book, I read her the book, I told them the story, I bought her the book.* Direct and indirect objects can cause trouble for some English speakers since they are often distinguished in English only by word order; as a rule of thumb, if a sentence appears to have two objects, the object that can be made part of a *to*-phrase without changing the meaning of the sentence is the indirect object.

Ман ба вай китобро додам, 'I gave him the book.'
Ман ба вай китобро хондам,
'I read her the book, I read the book to her.'

However, English sometimes uses an indirect object where Tajiki would not. Use of the Tajiki indirect object indicates that the person *has actually received* the object or *experienced* the action, whereas English can use the indirect object with some verbs to indicate someone *for whose benefit* the action was performed even if that person didn't receive anything; these are usually distinguished by the terms "recipient" and "beneficiary." The beneficiary indirect object is indicated in English by the preposition *for*, as in the equivalent sentences *I bought her a book* (indirect object pronoun) and *I bought a book for her* (prepositional phrase). The beneficiary is indicated in Tajiki with the preposition **барои**.

> **Ман китобро <u>барои вай</u> харидам**,
> 'I bought <u>her</u> the book, I bought the book <u>for her</u>.'
> **Ман номаро <u>барои вай</u> навиштам**,
> 'I wrote the letter <u>for him</u>.'
> (*Compare this with the following:*
> **Ман <u>ба вай</u> нома навиштам**,
> 'I wrote <u>him</u> a letter, a letter <u>to him</u>.')

Note that a sentence may well have both a beneficiary and a recipient:

> **Ман *барои вай* <u>ба падараш</u> нома навиштам**,
> 'I wrote a letter <u>to her father</u> *for her*, I wrote <u>her father</u> a letter *for her*.'
> **Ман *ба Дилбар* *барои додараш* китоб додам**,
> 'I gave <u>Dilbar</u> a book *for her younger brother*.'

Besides the beneficiary, **барои** is also used to indicate the purpose or the object of an action, also indicated by *for* in English.

> **Ман барои сабзавот ба мағоза рафтам**,
> 'I went to the store for vegetables.'
> **беморхона барои ветеранҳо**,
> 'hospital for veterans' (*though the phrase*
> **беморхонаи ветеранҳо** *'veterans' hospital' is preferred*)

However, you should not automatically translate *for* with **барои**, since *for* has a very wide variety of meanings in English that are conveyed in several different ways in Tajiki. The most important uses of *for* besides beneficiary and purpose are the following.

Distance: To indicate extent or distance traveled, Tajiki does not use a preposition.

Мо се километр давидем, 'We ran (for) three kilometers.'

Duration: To indicate the amount of time passed in an activity, just use the amount of time without a preposition.

Ман се соат кор кардам, 'I worked for three hours.'
Ман се соат кор мекунам, 'I'll work for three hours.'

When the activity is still continuing in the present, however, you can put the amount of time at the beginning of the sentence followed by **аст, ки**..., or else follow the amount of time by the adverb **боз** 'still.'

Ду соат аст, ки ман давида истодаам,
'I've been running for two whole hours'
(literally, 'It's two hours that I've run/I'm running').
Ман ду соат боз давида истодаам,
'I've been running for two hours.'

Exchange: When exchanging, buying, or selling things, *for* indicates what was traded or paid for something. In this sense Tajiki uses **ба**.

Ман ин халтаи себро ба як доллар гирифтам,
'I got this bag of apples for a dollar.'

Substitution: When substituting for someone or something else, the substitutee is indicated by **ба чои** 'in place of' with izofat or a personal possessive marker. (This is usually indicated by *in place of* or *instead of* in English; **ба чояш** often simply means *instead*.)

Ман ба чояш рафтам, 'I went for her = I went in her place.'
Ман ба чойи падарам кор кардам,
'I worked for my father = I substituted for my father at work.'
Парвиз ба чойи қаҳва чой дам кард,
'Parviz made tea for (instead of) coffee.'

Restriction: When *for* is used to indicate a class or group for comparison in the sense of "considering" (for example, *It's pretty tasty for rum*/*considering that it's rum*), Tajiki uses **дар** 'in, at.' (Note that Tajiki treats this usage in the same way as the usage of **дар** to indicate the respect in which a quality holds true.)

> **Дар ин синнусол Далер хеле боақл аст,**
> 'Daler is very smart for this (his) age.'

The stronger sense of "despite" indicated by *for all* (*For all his wealth, he still buys lottery tickets*) is translated with **новобаста ба**:

> **Новобаста ба синнусолаш Далер хеле бофаҳм аст,**
> 'For all his youth, Daler is very wise.'

Role: *For* is often used to indicate the role something serves in a customary schedule or a certain arrangement (*For starters, we'll go on a picnic; That'll have to do for a big finish*); this is especially common with food at meals. In this sense Tajiki uses **дар**.

> **Онҳо дар наҳорӣ тухм хӯрданд,** 'They ate eggs for breakfast.'

Favoring: Where English uses *for* and *against*, Tajiki uses **тарафдор** 'supporter' and **зид** 'contrary,' though to indicate support of a team **ҳаводор** 'fan' is used. There are many other idiomatic uses of *for* in English whose Tajiki equivalents you will have to learn individually.

e. The preposition то. The basic English equivalent of **то** is 'until'; more precisely, **то** is used to indicate the point up to which a condition holds, a movement takes place, or an action occurs. Thus, it is often equivalent to 'up to,' 'as far as,' or 'by':

> **то Душанбе** 'until Dushanbe'
> **то рӯзи душанбе** 'until/by Monday'
> **то саҳифа чилу панҷ** 'up to page 45'
> **то пагоҳ** 'until tomorrow,'
> **то боздид / то дидан** 'until we meet again'
> (*all commonly said when people part*)

In addition, **то** can be used instead of **аз** 'than' with comparatives. When used as a conjunction, **то** has a wide range of meanings depending on the tense of the verb in its subordinate clause; see Chapter 5, Section 6.

f. The prepositions чуз and ғайри. These two prepositions are much the same in meaning, 'except.' Also common are the compound prepositions **ба чуз, ба ғайр,** and **ғайр аз,** similar in meaning but more emphatic.

g. The prepositions бар and фар. The preposition **бар** 'over, above' indicates location; it can mean both *on top of* (touching) and *above* (not touching). The preposition **фар** 'down' is not used in modern spoken Tajiki; it is sometimes encountered in poetry. It is, however, an important prefix for verbs.

7. Equational and existential sentences

The simplest kinds of sentences in Tajiki are equational and existential sentences. *Equational* sentences are those with a form of the verb 'to be' like *John is American, Saadi was a great poet,* and *Anusha is not tall*; in such sentences, one nominal (the subject) is equated with, grouped with, or described as another nominal (the complement). *Existential* sentences are those with a form of 'there is' like *There are lots of plates in the washer, There were many people there,* and *There isn't a lot to do here*; existential sentences state that a certain nominal exists (or does not exist), usually in a particular location. Equational and existential sentences differ from each other in the present tense (but not in the negative), in which tense they use slightly irregular verb forms. (In other tenses the verb forms are regular and will be discussed later.)

Equational sentences are formed with the predicate endings, a set of endings agreeing with the subject in person and number that are added to the last nominal in the sentence, corresponding to the copula *am/is/are* of English. The predicate endings are underlined in the following sentences, which show the form they take following a consonant; note that the 3rd person singular predicate ending **аст** is not written joined to the preceding word.

	Singular	Plural
1st	Ман бемор<u>ам</u>, 'I am ill'	Мо бемор<u>ем</u>, 'We are ill'
2nd	Ту бемор<u>ӣ</u>, 'You are ill'	Шумо бемор<u>ед</u>, 'You are ill'
3rd	Ӯ/ Вай/Он бемор <u>аст</u>, 'He/she is ill'	Онҳо бемор<u>анд</u>, 'They are ill'

If the predicate endings are added to a word ending in a vowel, a **й** is automatically added to break up the sequence of vowels, which causes the 1ˢᵗ singular and 3ʳᵈ plural endings **ам** and **анд** to be written **ям** and **янд**. In the *literary* language, following a vowel **аст** often loses its initial **а** and contracts with the preceding word, so that **кӣ аст** 'who is?' and **чӣ аст** 'what is?' are often pronounced (and written) **кист/чист**. However, in the *colloquial* language **аст** is always omitted.

Equational sentences have the general basic form:

Noun phrase/ Pronoun *Subject*	Noun/Adjective phrase *Complement*	Personal Ending *Copula 'to be'*

Он пиёла аст, 'That is a bowl.'
Он пиёла калон аст, 'That bowl is large.'
Он пиёлаи калон аст, 'That is a large bowl.'
Дилбару Зулфия хоҳаранд, 'Dilbar and Zulfia are sisters.'
Дилбару Зулфия муаллиманд, 'Dilbar and Zulfia are teachers.'

It is considered very awkward to use the predicate endings immediately after the personal possessive markers; usually the personal possessive marker is replaced by an izofat phrase with the personal pronoun, though one may also use an alternate copular verb (see Chapter 3, Section 7.1).

The verb **ҳаст** is used to form existential sentences. It is conjugated as follows; although it can take any subject, it occurs most commonly in the 3ʳᵈ person. Note that except in the 3ʳᵈ person singular its endings are the same as the predicate endings, which is generally true of all the personal endings of Tajiki verbs.

	Singular	*Plural*
1ˢᵗ	**ҳастам** 'I exist'	**ҳастем** 'we exist'
2ⁿᵈ	**ҳастӣ** 'you (*sg.*) exist'	**ҳастед** 'you (*pl.*) exist'
3ʳᵈ	**ҳаст** 'there is'	**ҳастанд** 'there are'

You should keep in mind that some Tajiks use **ҳаст** in equational sentences in place of the predicate endings, especially for emphasis. This is considered substandard and you should avoid it.

An existential sentence in its basic form contains a noun phrase or pronoun as subject, a prepositional phrase of location (which is not necessary when simply asserting the existence or non-existence of the subject), and the appropriate form of the verb **ҳаст**. The prepositional phrase is often placed before the subject.

Дар ин боғ гули наргис ҳаст,
'There are narcissus flowers in this garden.'
Note: *Plural inanimates and nouns for small plants usually take a singular verb ending.*

The present negative of **ҳаст** is formed with the word **нест** 'there is not' and the same endings as **ҳаст** takes:

Ман сер нестам, 'I am not full.'
Мо сер нестем, 'We are not full.'
Ту сер нестӣ, 'You (*sg.*) are not full.'
Шумо сер нестед, 'You (*pl.*) are not full.'
Ӯ (вай) сер нест, 'He/she is not full.'
Онҳо сер нестанд, 'They are not full.'
Дар инҷо нон нест, 'There's no bread here.'
Ин нон нест, 'This isn't bread.'

In *formal* Tajiki, the appropriate form of **нест** is also used to form the negative of an *equational* sentence containing a predicate ending; thus, the negative of **Ман муаллимам** 'I am a teacher' is **Ман муаллим нестам** 'I am not a teacher.' However, in *colloquial* Tajiki the negative of an equational sentence is formed by adding **не** to the end of the sentence and omitting the predicate ending entirely: **Ман муаллим не** 'I am not a teacher.' In classical Persian, the negative of the predicate endings was formed regularly with the prefix **на-**: **наям** 'I am not,' **най** 'you are not,' **наяст** 'he is not,' **наем** 'we are not,' etc. This usage can be found in poetry.

The simple interrogative (yes/no form) of all types of sentences is shown by intonation. The word order remains the same.

Шумо хастаед? 'Are you tired?'
Мо ташнаем? 'Are we thirsty?'
Ӯ гурусна аст? 'Is he hungry?'
Шумо зебоед? 'Are you beautiful?'
Он китоб аст? 'Is it a book?'

Онҳо шоданд? 'Are they happy?'
Вай хаста нест? 'Isn't he tired?'
Ту гушна нестӣ? 'Aren't you hungry?'
Нон ҳаст? 'Is there bread?'
Нон нест? 'Isn't there bread?'

Chapter 3   Verbs

1. Overview of the Tajiki verb

The central part of a sentence in terms of meaning is the verb; in fact, in Tajiki it is possible for a complete sentence to consist of only a verb. In broad terms, a sentence describes an event, a set of circumstances, or a state of affairs. The verb names the state, change of state, or action described by the sentence, while the subject, objects, and most prepositional phrases name the various people, things, and places involved in what the sentence describes (called its *participants*). English and Tajiki are very similar in the ways they name states and actions with verbs and how they classify participants by the grammatical functions they fill. However, in Tajiki the distinction between events and changes of state on the one hand and states on the other is somewhat more important than in English, and for some verbs the participants are not given the same grammatical roles in English and Tajiki.

In colloquial Tajiki the verb is the last word in the sentence (except for certain interrogative particles, which are often clitics and thus act as part of the verb). This was not true in earlier centuries, however, so in much classical Persian poetry word order in a sentence was much freer; in poetry, certain set phrases, and songs the verb often is not the last word in a sentence (just as English word order is more variable there).

In general, the Tajiki verb is grammatically similar to but easier than the English verb: Most Tajiki verb forms are formed regularly from the basic verb forms with prefixes, endings, and auxiliary verbs, and the basic forms of a Tajiki verb are simpler than in English. In English a verb generally has three forms that a foreign student must learn (its *principle parts*), the present, simple past, and past participle (for example, *sing/sang/sung*); all other forms of most verbs are based on these forms. In Tajiki almost all verbs have only two principle parts, the past stem (or infinitive) and the present stem. The verbs доштан 'to have,' будан 'to be,' ҳаст 'there is/are,' and нест 'to not be, there is/are not' are major exceptions.

The past stem always ends in д (following vowels and voiced consonants) or т (following voiceless consonants): хонд (хондан 'to read'), **истод** (**истодан** 'to stand') **хост** (**хостан** 'to want'); the infinitive is formed from the past stem simply by adding **-ан**. Unfortunately for the foreign learner, the present stem is not easily determined from the past stem for many verbs; it is an independent form that for many verbs must be memorized. Historically the past tense stem was formed from the present stem by adding one of a small number of suffixes; however, because of changes over the millennia in the pronunciation of Tajiki consonants depending on neighboring sounds, the past and present stems have diverged for many verbs and a system of consonant mutations has come into being. Thus, there are a number of general patterns relating the past and present stems that hold for many verbs, but they have many exceptions.

The most regular pattern is that the past stem is formed from the present stem by suffixing **-д** or **-ид**; this is the formation used for almost all denominal verbs (verbs formed from nouns), for example: **рақс** 'dance' (borrowed from Arabic), **ме-рақс-ам** 'I dance,' **рақс-ид-ам** 'I danced,' and **тарс** 'fear,' **ме-тарс-ам** 'I fear,' **тарс-ид-ам** 'I feared.' It is also the pattern for many native Tajiki verbs, such as **хондан/хон** 'to read,' **хӯрдан/хӯр** 'to eat,' and **мондан/мон** 'to put.' (Verbs will be given by their infinitives, followed by their present stem if necessary, as above: **хостан/хоҳ** 'to want.') Note that some verbs have infinitives in both **-дан** and **-идан**, usually with no difference in meaning: **парвар(и)дан/парвар** 'to foster, to to train,.'

Verbs with past stems ending in **-од**, **-ид**, and **-ист** usually form their present stems by dropping the suffix: **истодан/ист** 'to stand,' **харидан/хар** 'to buy,' **донистан/дон** 'to know.'

The following are four of the most common less regular patterns for past and present stems.

	Pres. Stem	*Infinitive*
1) з/хт:	соз	сохтан 'to build'
	рез	рехтан 'to pour'
2) б/фт:	ёб	ёфтан 'to find'
	коб	кофтан 'to look for'
3) о/уд:	намо	намудан 'to seem, appear'
	рабо	рабудан 'to seize'

However, for many verbs there has been so much change in the sounds of the language over the millennia that there remain no regular patterns relating the past and present stems; examples include **бурдан/бар** 'to carry,' **мурдан/мир** 'to die' (though a regular present stem **мур** is also commonly used), **кардан/кун** 'to do,' **додан/диҳ** 'to give,' **нишастан/(ни)шин** 'to sit,' **шунидан/шунав** 'to hear,' and **задан/зан** 'to hit.' (Indeed, for some verbs a regular present stem created from the past stem coexists with an older, irregular present stem, as with **мурдан/мир~мур** 'to die' mentioned above; for other verbs an older irregular past stem and a newer regular one formed from the present stem coexist, such as **ҷастан~ҷаҳидан/ҷаҳ** 'to jump, leap.' This process of creating regular forms to replace irregular ones is called *back-formation* by linguists.) For a very few verbs, the past and present stems come from unrelated verbs, like *be/am/was* and *go/went* in English. (This is called *suppletion* by linguists.) Thus, the predicate endings and **ҳаст** form their other tenses with **будан**, and the present stem of **дидан** 'to see' is **бин**.

On the other hand, Tajiki is more complex than English in that the verb has a full set of endings that agree with the subject in person and number; however, in all tenses they are the same as the predicate endings except in the third person singular (*he, she, it*). (In addition, in colloquial Tajiki the verb can take a second suffix indicating the direct or indirect object of the sentence.) The personal ending of the verb does not agree in number with the subject in two cases: First, to show respect to an elder or superior, the plural verb endings are used in the 2nd and 3rd persons. Second, plural subjects that are inanimate (including small plants) usually take a singular verb ending.

Not all Tajiki verbs can take all tense forms. Verbs that name states of being, like 'to have,' 'to be able,' and 'to want,' cannot form tenses indicating on-going activities, that is, continuous tense forms or those with the prefix **ме-** apart from the present-future tense.

All verbs except **ҳаст** and **нест** form the negative with the prefix **на-**, which always takes primary stress.

2. Transitivity, direct objects, and definiteness

There is a further distinction for verbs that requires more attention in Tajiki than in English, *transitivity*. Transitive verbs are those that take a direct object (*eat, make, extract*, etc.); intransitive verbs only have a subject (*be, seem, fall*, etc.). In English many transitive verbs can be used quite freely intransitively as well. Thus, *John's eating dinner* (transitive) and *John's eating* (intransitive), or *The man's hang-*

ing the coat on the hook (transitive) and *The coat's hanging on the hook* (intransitive). In Tajiki, on the other hand, almost all verbs are either transitive or intransitive but not both (exceptions include **мондан/ мон** 'to remain; to put, place'), and you must learn whether a verb is transitive or intransitive along with its meaning and its two principle parts; quite often, however, corresponding transitive and intransitive verbs are closely related in form or else one is derived regularly from the other. (This is discussed more fully in Section 7.5 below.)

As mentioned before, the direct object is generally marked in Tajiki with **-ро** if it is definite and unmarked if it is indefinite; however, definiteness is a complex matter in any language and what is considered definite or indefinite often varies somewhat between languages. In English, the basic rule of thumb is that a noun is definite if it is a proper name or if it is modified by a demonstrative or the definite article *the*; indefinite nouns are modified by the indefinite articles *a/an/some*, or else are plural common nouns without an article. As far as meaning is concerned, a definite noun has just been mentioned or refers to something concrete that is being pointed to or is immediately clear from the context. In English grammar it is customary to say that *the* points to a unique, exclusive person, place, or thing, while *a/an* implies that there are others of that noun as well, but this is only true when talking about singular nouns. The basic meaning of *definite* is that the object or objects named by the noun are identifiable or predictable from context: In *The man who just came in is my lawyer*, the man can be identified, picked out from a crowd, and considered known to the listener. On the other hand, in *I went to a wedding yesterday and the bride wore purple*, the listener is not able to identify the bride if he passes her on the street or sees her in a crowd, but the fact that there was a wedding implies there must have been a bride. (These basic types of definiteness are called *identifiable* and *familiar* by linguists.)

In general, definiteness is as important in Tajiki as in English but, because Tajiki does not have a definite article, it is usually indicated indirectly, except in constructions that automatically make a noun definite or indefinite. Even more confusing for English learners, nouns that are marked as definite in certain constructions become indeterminate in definiteness if these constructions are used in certain specific circumstances. For example, while **-ро** indicates a definite direct object most of the time, in certain circumstances (when the noun is modified by a relative clause, for example, or when the direct object is placed before the subject) it does not indicate definiteness at all but only that the noun is the direct object of the main clause. In such cases we will say that the construction is *formally definite* but *actually indefinite*, for example.

Now, in most Tajiki sentences the direct object follows the subject, in which case **-ро** indicates that the noun is definite. Thus, **Ӯ китобро хонд** 'She read the book,' **Ман ӯро дидам** 'I saw her.' A noun or noun phrase without **-ро** (in general, the simple noun whenever it is unmodified) is indefinite (either singular or plural) and often generic, as in English sentences like *He hunts deer, She buys books,* or *They grow cotton,* in which the noun indicates a general category of things, often associated with habitual or occupational actions. (In the corresponding Tajiki sentences it can be hard to distinguish such an indefinite object from part of a compound verb.) Thus, **Ӯ китоб хонд** can mean 'She read a book,' 'She read some books,' 'She read books (habitually),' or even 'She studied (at that time).'

To indicate that the noun is indefinite but not generic, you can use the indefinite marker **-е** or the numeral **як** 'one': **Ӯ як китоб овард**, 'She brought a book.' (When indicating indefiniteness, **-е** is literary and would not be used in colloquial speech. However, it is routinely used in colloquial speech in its other uses, which will be discussed later.)

Ман се кило себ харидам, 'I bought three kilos of apples.'
Ман себ гирифтам, 'I got an apple/apples.'
Ман себро гирифтам, 'I got the apple.'
Ман он себро гирифтам, 'I got that apple.'

However, it is possible to put the direct object before the subject for emphasis or contrast. In this case the direct object is *formally* definite and must take **-ро** but can be indefinite *in sense*, which is shown by the indefinite clitic **-е** or the numeral **як** 'one' in conjunction with **-ро**, which simply indicates the direct object: **Як китобро вай овард, як китобро ман овардам**, '*She* brought a book and *I* brought a book/so did I.'

Себро ман гирифтам, 'I got the apple/an apple/apples.'
Як себро ман гирифтам, 'I got an apple.'

Similarly, *indefinite plural nouns* can be indicated by **чанд** 'several' or **ягон** 'some,' which indicate that the speaker has specific books or instances of reading in mind; the simple plural would be nonspecific but would not be generic. *Specific* nouns are those whose identity the speaker has in mind, though the listener does not or is not expected to; *non-specific* nouns are those whose actual identity is unknown to the speaker. Indefinite nouns can be either specific or nonspecific, which is the difference in English between "I'm looking for a French book; do you have one?" (non-specific) and "I'm looking for a French book; do you have it?" (specific). (Another word for 'several,' **якчанд**, differs from **чанд** in being definite, and thus requiring -**ро**.) Thus:

Ӯ чанд китоб овард, 'She was brought some (particular) books.'
Ӯ китоб мехонд, 'She was reading books (habitually).'
 but:
Ӯ якчанд китобро мехонд, 'She was reading several books.'

Note that the following types of direct object are always considered definite by Tajiki grammar (formally definite) and thus should always take -**ро**:

1) Demonstrative pronouns
Ман дирӯз инро дидам, 'I saw this yesterday.'
Шумо онро харидед? 'Did you buy that?'

2) Nouns modified by demonstrative adjectives:
Ин қаламро гир! 'Take this pencil!'
Он мардро тамошо кун! 'Watch that man!'

3) Personal pronouns
ман, ту, вай, мо, шумо, онҳо, etc.;

4) Proper names
Зарафшон, Карим, Хатлон, etc.:
Ман парерӯз кино тамошо кардам,
'The day before yesterday I watched a movie.'
Ман парерӯз кинои "Рустам ва Сӯҳроб"-ро тамошо кардам,
'The day before yesterday I watched the movie *Rustam and Suhrob*.'

5) Nouns modified by relative clauses
Мо аллакай китоберо, ки дар рӯи миз аст, хондаем,
'We have already read the book that is on the table.'

Some of these types of direct object can logically be indefinite (for example, *I saw a man who told me where you went*); in this case, **-ро** must still be used to indicate that the phrase is the direct object of the sentence, but the sense of indefiniteness is indicated explicitly by such words as **як** 'one.' Thus, to summarize, the learner should keep in mind that while the clitics **-е** and **-ро** are always *formally* indefinite and definite, respectively, in many constructions they serve other grammatical functions and then are not necessarily either *actually* definite or indefinite. Actual definiteness or indefiniteness is then shown if necessary by other independent words (**он, якчанд, ягон**, etc.), and otherwise must be determined from context.

The precise sense of **-е** and **-ро** in conjunction can be quite subtle. For example, consider the following four questions, all of which mean 'What books did you read?'

A. **Чӣ китобҳо-е-ро хондед?**
B. **Чӣ китобҳо-е хондед?**
C. **Чӣ китобҳо-ро хондед?**
D. **Чӣ китобҳо хондед?**

The first points to note are that an inanimate noun, **китоб** 'book,' is in the plural, so both speaker and hearer know that more than one book is in question (or that this is a reasonable expectation given the conversation thus far), and the fact that the plurality of an inanimate noun is used means that a fairly representative listing of books one has read is probably expected; and **чӣ** 'what?' can be either definite or indefinite depending on context (whereas **кадом** 'which?' is always definite). Thus, the exact sense of each question must be determined from context and by contrast with each of the other questions, given the points above.

Now, B and D (without **-ро**) are almost identical in connotation; a plural inanimate noun indicates little more than that the group of things in question has more than one member, while the indefinite marker does not materially alter this. Going beyond this, the use of **-ро** adds a certain sort of definiteness or specific character to B or D, but the details depend to some extent on context. Comparing A and B (both with **-е**), the former (with **-ро**) means that the set of books, or at least the broad range of books one might expect, is known, but the exact books read are not known; *that* is what exactly is being asked. A is the question one would ask of someone who studied in a particular program in college, for example, B of someone who has simply read a lot.

Comparing A and C (with **-po**), the difference is that in A (with **-e**), the focus is broader than in C: In A, a wider variety of books is expected, say books from different genres or from throughout a field to get a feel for the breadth of one's reading, whereas in C a narrower range of books is expected, say to get a feel for one's depth of study in a particular area. Presumably A is the question one would ask, say, about the readings in a degree program and C what one would ask about a particular class.

Thus, in this case **-po** indicates roughly whether a natural or coherent set is expected or not, while the use of **-e** serves to broaden the focus or relevance of the question within those limits.

Now, if you are beginning your study of Tajiki, you should not worry about being able to catch all these distinctions yourself, much less being able to produce them in your speech; they are very subtle and depend a great deal on context, and understanding them fluently requires much experience. However, you *should* take note of the variability in the exact senses of **-e** and **-po** as you encounter them (especially when used together) and pay attention to the contexts in which they're used.

3. Personal possessive markers as object suffixes

In Tajiki, as you have learned, definite direct objects are indicated with **-po** and indirect objects with prepositions. However, direct and indirect objects can also be indicated by using the personal possessive markers as object endings on the verb; the object ending comes after the person-number ending for the subject and must agree with the omitted direct object in person and number. For example, in the sentence **Вай моро дид,** 'He saw us,' the direct object **моро** can be replaced by the object suffix **-амон: Вай дидамон,** 'He saw us.' It is generally possible to omit the subject pronoun, so this sentence will often be simply **Дидамон,** 'He saw us.' Note however that the verb **дидам** is ambiguous by itself; it can mean either 'I saw' or 'he saw me.' In this case (simple past with 1st singular ending), the subject is usually not omitted.

Ман туро дидам / (Ман) дидамат, 'I saw you.'
Ту маро дидӣ / (Ту) дидиям, 'You saw me.'
Вайҳо шуморо мешунаванд / (Вайҳо) мешунавандатон,
'They will hear you.'

Дар Париж харидедашон? 'Did you buy them in Paris?'

If the sentence has both a direct and an indirect object, the object ending must refer to the indirect object.

Ман ба ӯ китобро додам, 'I gave him the book.'
= **(Ман) китобро додамаш.**
Ман ба ӯ мегӯям, 'I'll tell her.'
= **Мегӯямаш.**

In addition, if the direct object has a personal possessive marker, the object ending is omitted if it would be the same. Thus, it is perfectly fine to say **Ман китобамро додамаш**, 'I gave her my book' and **Ман китобатро додамаш,** 'I gave her your book.' If the direct object belongs to the recipient, the recipient is effectively indicated on the direct object and not on the verb.

Ман китобашро додам, 'I gave her her book.'
Вай китобамро дод, 'She gave me my book.'

If the recipient is third person and the direct object is owned by another third person who is known from the context (so that if the ending **-аш** would refer to two different people if repeated), either the possessor or the recipient must be explicitly mentioned in the sentence:

Ман китоби падарамро додамаш, 'I gave him my father's book.'
Ман ба падарам китобашро додам, 'I gave my father his book'
Note: *that is, someone else's book, if the book has already been discussed and its owner clear from context; otherwise it means the book belongs to my father.*

For first and second person subjects, the object suffix cannot be of the same person. Thus, *****Дидамам** 'I saw me' is ungrammatical, as are *****Дидемам** 'We saw me,' *****Дидият** 'You (*sg.*) saw you (*sg.*),' *****Дидедатон** 'You (*pl.*) saw you (*pl.*),' and so on. It is possible for a verb to have both third person subject and object, but in that case they can only refer to different people. Thus, it is not possible to replace the reflexive or reciprocal pronouns with an object suffix.

Дидаш, 'He saw him' (*someone else*)
Худашро дид, 'He saw himself.'
Задандашон, 'They hit them' (*another group*)

Худашонро заданд, 'They hit themselves.'
Якдигарро заданд, 'They hit each other.'

As mentioned in the section on personal possessive markers, in colloquial Tajiki the personal possessive markers have distinct direct object forms due to fusion with **-а**, the reduced form of **-ро**; these forms are also used as object markers, in which case forms like **дидам** are not ambiguous: **дидам** 'I saw,' **дидма** 'he saw me.'

4. Simple, prefixed, and compound verbs

There are three broad classes of verbs in Tajiki, simple, prefixed, and compound verbs. Simple verbs are ones which are not composed of any smaller independent words, such as **будан** 'to be,' **гуфтан** 'to say, speak,' **омадан** 'to come,' and **кардан** 'to do.'

Prefixed verbs are verbs (usually verbs of motion) to which prefixes like **фар, бар,** or **дар** have been added, usually to indicate the direction in which the motion is carried out; **бар** generally indicates motion outwards and **дар** motion inwards, as in the pair of verbs **баромадан/баро** 'to come out' and **даромадан/даро** 'to come in.' Most prefixed verbs are inseparable: The prefix is fused to the verb root and other verbal prefixes (the negative and continuous aspect markers) precede it. However, a few prefixed verbs are separable, in which case the other verbal prefixes come between it and the verb root; common separable prefixed verbs include **вохӯрдан** 'to meet, come across' (from **хӯрдан** 'to eat'), **бозгаштан** 'to return, come back' (from **гаштан** 'to turn, spin'), and **даргирифтан** 'to catch on fire, come alight' (from **гирифтан** 'to take, get'). For all prefixed verbs, separable or inseparable, the prefix is always written joined to the following verb form and never takes the stress.

Compound verbs (more precisely, *nominal-compound verbs*) include a noun before a simple verb; they are very common in Tajiki. The most common verbs used in compound verbs are **кардан** 'to do,' **доштан** 'to have,' **шудан** 'to become,' and **мондан** 'to put, remain': **кор кардан** 'to work' (from **кор** 'work'), **сар кардан** 'to start' (from **сар** 'head'), **дӯст доштан** 'to like' (from **дӯст** 'friend'). In the infinitive and most other verb forms, the noun in a compound verb is written separately from the verb and precedes any verbal prefixes.

CHAPTER 3 - Verbs

5. Verb tense forms

There are several categories of meaning that Tajiki verbs show through their form; in general they are very similar to corresponding categories in English. They are tense proper, composed of time and aspect; voice; mood; and evidentiality.

1) **Time** — the time an action or change of state occurred or a state held good relative to the time of speaking: Past, present, future.

2) **Aspect** — the way the "internal make-up" of an action is viewed: Continuous (ongoing or in progress *at a given time*, like the English progressive), imperfect (occurring continuously *throughout a stretch of time*), habitual (occurring repeatedly *throughout a stretch of time*), perfect (completed *by a given time*), or simple (undifferentiated).

2) **Voice** — the way that the grammatical roles that the logical subject and logical direct object play in an event are assigned by the verb form: Active, passive, and causative. (English only has the first two voices.)

4) **Mood** — the degree of actuality, possibility, or desirability of an action: Indicative (indicating an actual, factual event or occurrence), subjunctive (indicating an event or occurrence that is not real but only possible, potential, or contingent on other events), imperative (indicating a command), probable. The probable mood is not treated here, and the subjunctive is commoner in Tajiki than English.

5) **Evidentiality** — whether the speaker has first-hand knowledge in speaking or is relying on the testimony of others (reportative). (In fact, the reportative is usually not indicated by distinct verb forms but instead uses perfect verb forms in other aspects.)

In addition to verb forms proper (finite verb forms), a Tajiki verb has a verbal noun (the infinitive), three verbal adjectives (the past, present, and future participles), and a verbal adverb. That is, they retain some verbal force, such as indicating the direct or indirect object of the action; in this respect the infinitive is different from *deverbal* nouns, which simply name some aspect of the action of the verb. These will be described and discussed along with the finite forms of the verb progressing in the order best suited for English learners in the active voice and indicative mood; the forms for a given tense in other voices and moods are very easily obtained from the active indicative form.

5.1 Non-finite verbs forms

a. Infinitives. Infinitives are nouns formed from verbs which serve to name the action of the verb. In English there are two verbal nouns, the infinitive, *to do*, and the gerund, *doing*, which have slightly different senses: The infinitive names the fact or the general idea of the action, while the gerund names the actual performance of the action. In Tajiki there is only one verbal noun, the infinitive, which is used in some of the uses of both of the English verbal nouns; however, there are other uses of the English infinitive and gerund that must be expressed in Tajiki with a subordinate clause (like English *I saw that he had left*). In many of their uses in English, infinitives and gerunds have logical subjects (though they are not expressed as grammatical subjects): *His singing bothers me* (gerund, subject indicated with the possessive), *I want her to sing* (infinitive, subject indicated with object pronoun), etc. In Tajiki, either the logical subject or the object of an infinitive is indicated by the personal possessive marker: **давиданам** 'my running,' **заданашон** 'their beating' (which can be a beating they either gave or received; the English is ambiguous in the same way as the Tajiki) or with an izofat construction: **рақсидани рақкоса** 'the dancer's dancing.' However, the Tajiki infinitive cannot indicate both the subject and the object (for example, there is no direct Tajiki equivalent to 'their beating me'); to express both, one must use a subordinate clause (see Chapter 5, Section 2).

The following are the most common uses of the infinitive and gerund in English with the corresponding constructions in Tajiki.

1) In English, one may use the infinitive or the gerund as the subject of a sentence, with very slight differences in meaning; the Tajiki infinitive is used for this:

Омӯхтани забони тоҷикӣ хеле осон аст,
'Learning Tajiki is very easy.'

Давидан ба ман маъқул аст,
'I like running.' (literally, 'Running interests me.')

In English, only the gerund can serve as the object of a preposition or the direct object of a sentence; this function is filled by the Tajiki infinitive:

Ман аз таб кардани писарам хавотирам,
'I'm worried about my son's running a fever.'
Суруд хонданаш ба ман маъқул нашуд,
'I didn't like her singing.'

2) English verbs of sensing can take gerund or infinitive objects (the infinitive in this case does not have "to"), with a slight difference in meaning: *I saw him running* focuses on the action that was actually in progress when I saw him, while *I saw him run* focuses on the completed event or summarizes the end result. The former is indicated in Tajiki with an object clause (see Chapter 5, Section 2) and the verb in one of the continuous tenses (discussed below), the latter with an infinitive, as in 2 above:

Ман дидам, ки ӯ давида истода буд,
'I saw him running' (literally, 'I saw that he was running')
Ман давиданашро дидам,
'I saw him run' (literally, 'I saw his running')

3) In English, the infinitive is used to indicate the purpose of an action: *I went to see him.* In Tajiki one uses a subordinate clause of purpose with **ки** 'that, so that' or **то ки** 'in order that' and the verb in the subjunctive (see Section 2.3b below): **Ман рафтам, ки вайро бинам**, 'I went to see him' (literally, 'I went that I might see him').

4) In English, the infinitive and gerund are used to name a verb that is the object of another verb: *I want to go, he loves sleeping.* There are a variety of corresponding constructions in Tajiki depending on the verbs in question. For example, the Tajiki equivalent of *want* + infinitive is a modal verb construction (similar to *I can go, I should go*, etc.) discussed in Section 6.2 below.

b. Past participle. The past participle is formed by dropping the final **-н** from the infinitive, or, alternatively, by adding **-а** to the past tense stem (the usual description among Tajik grammarians). It is an adjective indicating that the action of the verb is completed, corresponding to the English *-ed* or *-en* verb forms (*bothered, woken, sung*, etc.); because it is an adjective, the stress falls on the final **-a**:

гузаштан 'to pass (of time)' > **гузашта** 'passed, past'

Similarly:
бастан 'to tie, bind' > **баста** 'closed'
мурдан 'to die' > **мурда** 'dead'
хӯрдан 'to eat' > **хӯрда** 'eaten'
гирифтан 'to take' > **гирифта** 'taken'
омадан 'to come' > **омада** 'come'
кушодан 'to open' > **кушода** 'open(ed)'
пухтан 'to cook' > **пухта** 'cooked'
дӯхтан 'to sew' > **дӯхта** 'sewn'

The past participle is often used where English would use a relative clause, in which case it is best thought of as meaning 'that was/had been…':

китоби хонда 'the book that was/had been read'
марди дида 'the man who was seen'
гапи гуфта 'the talk/words that had been spoken'
Ман ба онҳо меваи пухтаро додам,
'I gave them the fruit that had ripened.'

It is also often used as a noun to name the results of an action:

кардан 'to do' > **карда** 'what had been done.'

Past participles of compound verbs are formed the same way, with the noun written joined to the verb; primary stress falls on the final **-a**, and secondary stress falls on the last syllable of the noun:

дӯст доштан 'to like' > **дӯстдошта** 'favorite'

The negative is formed by prefixing **на-** (which takes the stress) to the verb. In the past participle of compound and separable prefixed verbs, **на-** falls between the noun and the verb; primary stress falls on **на-** and the noun retains secondary stress:

накарда 'that which had not been done'
дӯстнадошта 'unliked'   **вонахӯрда** 'unmet'

Because the past participle of non-compound verbs is fairly short, a **-гӣ** is added to it in colloquial Tajiki: **хондагӣ** 'read,' **нагуфтагӣ** 'unspoken.' However, adding **-гӣ** to *compound verbs* is optional. It is used adjectivally like the past participle:

хонаи рӯфтагӣ 'a clean-swept house'
кори шудагӣ 'completed work'
китоби нахондагӣ 'an unread book'
дари пӯшидагӣ 'a closed door'

In English a past participle can be used as an adjective only if it is formed from a simple verb phrase with at most an adverb: *a much-read book, a little-known restaurant, my car's well-oiled engine*; if the verb phrase is longer, it is made into a relative clause. In Tajiki, on the other hand, much longer verb phrases (particularly ones containing a prepositional phrase) can be made into a participle, in which case they are written as one word. Thus, from the phrase **аз нав оиладор шудан** 'to be married anew (**аз нав**), to be remarried' is formed the participle **азнавоиладоршуда** 'remarried,' which is treated as a simple adjective. Because such participles take a generic meaning, they cannot be formed from verb phrases containing a definite time or place reference, which are always written as separate words:

Ман шафтолуи дирӯз дидаамро харидам,
'I bought the peaches that I saw yesterday.'
Note: *the possessive ending is used to indicate the subject of the verb phrase that was made into a participle.*

In addition to its adjectival use, the past participle is quite commonly used to form a compound sentence, that is, one in which the subject is followed by more than one predicate. The past participle indicates a *completed* action (the first verb) *succeeded* by the action of the second verb; both verbs must have the same subject. (The long form in **-гӣ** cannot be used in this construction.) If the first action continues as the second begins, you cannot use the past participle; instead, the verbal adverb is often used (see Section e below). In such cases, the Tajiki past participle is similar to the English *present* participle. Compare the following:

Ҷавонон ба ошхона омаданд ва хӯрок хӯрданд.	The young people came to a restaurant and had dinner.	Ҷавонон ба ошхона омада, хӯрок хӯрданд.	Coming to a restaurant, the young people had dinner.
Ӯ китобро дар рӯйи миз гузошт ва аз хона баромад.	He/she put the book on the table and went out.	Ӯ китобро дар рӯйи миз гузошта, аз хона баромад.	Putting the book on the table, he/she went out.
Лола модарашро дид ва гуфт:	Lola met her mother and said…	Лола модарашро дида гуфт:	Meeting her mother, Lola said…

This construction is the basis for several verb tenses in which the second verb in the compound is an auxiliary verb; that is, the second verb has lost its meaning as a full verb and only serves to indicate a particular shade of meaning or grammatical function. Thus, **гирифтан** 'to take, get' is often used as an auxiliary to indicate doing an action once and for all: For example, from **навиштан** 'to write' is formed **навишта гирифтан** 'to write down.' Most importantly, certain verbs are used with the past participle of another verb to indicate the continuous tenses or passive voice.

c. **Present participle**. The present participle is formed differently for simple, compound, and prefixed verbs. For simple and prefixed verbs, the suffix **-анда** is added to the present stem of the verb (**-янда** after vowels). For compound verbs the present stem alone is used; the noun and present stem are written as one word:

Infinitive	*Present stem*	*Present participle*
навиштан	навис	нависанда 'writing *(adj.)*'
кардан	кун	кунанда 'doing *(adj.)*'
гуфтан	гӯй	гӯянда 'saying *(adj.)*'
омадан	о	оянда 'coming *(adj.)*'
баромадан	баро	барояанда 'coming out *(adj.)*'

вохӯрдан	вохӯр	вохӯранда 'meeting (adj.)'
кор кардан	кор кун	коркун 'working (adj.)'
моҳӣ гирифтан	моҳӣ гир	моҳигир 'fishing (adj.)'

The negative participle ends in -анда/-янда for all verbs; на- is prefixed to the entire verb form for simple verbs and prefixed verbs with inseparable prefixes, but after the prefix of separable prefixed verbs and after the noun of compound verbs: набароянда 'not coming out,' вонахӯранда 'not meeting,' корнакунанда 'not working.'

The present participle is an adjective used to indicate ongoing action; its basic translation is a relative clause, such as нависанда 'that/who is writing.' Thus, марди хӯранда 'the man who is eating, the eating man,' гурбаи даванда 'the cat that is running, the running cat,' ҳафтаи оянда 'the week that is coming, next week.' As with past participles, more complex present participial clauses can be used as compound adjectives, in which case all the words in the clause are customarily written together as one word. Also, present participles are frequently used as nouns indicating the doer of an action:

    нависанда 'writing (adj.); writer'
    гӯянда 'saying (adj.); speaker'
    сароянда 'singing (adj.); singer' (from сурудан/саро 'to sing')
    навозанда 'playing (adj.); player of musical instruments'
       (from навохтан/ навоз 'to play an instrument')
    шунаванда 'hearing (adj.); listener'
       (from шунидан/шунав 'to hear')
    моҳигир 'fishing (adj.); fisherman'
       (from моҳӣ 'fish' and гирифтан/гир 'to take, catch')
    даванда 'running (adj.); runner'
    дарсхон 'learner' (from дарс хондан/хон 'to study a lesson')
    коркун 'employee' (from кор кардан/кун 'to work')
    рӯзноманигор 'journalist'
       (from рӯзнома нигоштан/нигор 'to write for a newspaper')

The names of many professions and activities are formed from the present participle with the suffix -ӣ (-гӣ after vowels); in some cases, the noun has an idiomatic meaning:

    нависандагӣ 'the profession of writing'
    моҳигирӣ 'the occupation or hobby of fishing'

хонандагӣ 'the occupation of singing'
(a more common meaning than 'reading, studying')

d. Future participle. The future participle is an adjective formed by adding the suffix **-ӣ** to the infinitive:

гапи гуфтанӣ
'something to say, a conversation one ought to have'
китоби хонданӣ
'a book to read, a book one ought to read'

The negative is formed by prefixing **на-** to the verb form for simple and inseparable prefixed verbs (**нагуфтанӣ, набаромаданӣ**) and adding **на-** between a separable prefix or complement noun and the simple verb root (**вонахӯрданӣ, корнакарданӣ**).

The future participle is used in the same circumstances that the infinitive may be used adjectivally in English. This use indicates that something is supposed to be or is about to be acted on (*books to read, bills to pay, people to see, things to do*), and by extension something intended for or suited to a purpose (*a room to let, money to burn, something to ease the pain, music to chase the blues away*). That is, it indicates obligation, intention, purpose, or near futurity.

e. Verbal adverbs. The verbal adverb is a form of the verb used to subordinate that verb to the main verb of the sentence in order to indicate the manner in which it is carried out; it usually corresponds to a present participle in English, such as *He came running* and *Frowning, he said...*, that either comes immediately after the main verb or at the very beginning of the sentence (in which case it is set off from the rest of the sentence with a comma). For other verbs, the meaning is best conveyed by an adverb like *smilingly* or a phrase like *while speaking*. The verbal adverb generally comes immediately after the subject in Tajiki.

To form the verbal adverb, add the suffix **-он** to the present stem of the verb. The verbal adverb of compound verbs is written as one word. Thus:

Verb	Present stem	Verbal adverb
давидан	дав	давон 'running'
гуфтан	гӯй	гӯён 'saying'
табассум кардан	табассум кун	табассумкунон 'smiling(ly)'

рақс кардан	рақс кун	рақскунон	'dancing(ly)'
гиристан	гирй	гирён	'crying, weeping'
афтидан	афт	афтон	'falling'
пешпо хӯрдан	пешпо хӯр	пешпохӯрон	'stumbling'

The verbal adverb must be used for an action that is occurring at the same time as the main action; if the subordinated action is completed before the main action begins, you must use the past participle.

Лола гирён дарро боз кард, 'Crying, Lola opened the door.'
Мурод давон об овард, 'Running, Murod carried water.'
Ман табассумкунон ба ӯ нигоҳ кардам, 'Smiling, I looked at him.'
Мулло дуохонон тасбеҳ мешуморид, 'Praying (reciting prayers), the mullah would count the beads.'
(**дуо хондан** 'to pray, recite a prayer')

f. Deverbal nouns. Deverbal nouns are nouns formed from verbs to name some aspect of the action of the verb (such as the faculty for performing the action or the process or result of the action). The most common deverbal noun is formed from the present stem of the verb by adding the suffix **-иш**.

Verb   *Noun*
дидан/бин 'to see'   **биниш** 'sight'
омӯхтан/омӯз 'to study'   **омӯзиш** 'training, instruction'
чаҳидан/чаҳ 'to jump'   **чаҳиш** 'jump'

Many of these deverbal nouns can be used in turn to form compound verbs:

дониш омӯхтан 'to learn'
гардиш кардан 'to take a walk'
супориш додан 'to give an order'

Another common deverbal suffix, **-ор**, is added to the past stem of a verb to indicate someone who engages in that activity; thus, from **харидан/хар** 'to buy' is formed **харидор** 'buyer.' This suffix is virtually the same in meaning as the present participle used as the name of a profession or type of actor (for example, **фурӯшанда** 'seller').

g. Deverbal adjectives. The deverbal adjective is formed from the present stem of the verb by suffixing **-о**. This form indicates the possession of a quality inherent in the verb; it only occurs with a very small number of simple verbs, practically limited to the following nine:

Verb	*Verbal adjective*
тавонистан 'to be able'	**тавоно** 'capable'
хондан 'to read'	**хоно** 'legible'
доштан 'to have'	**доро** 'rich; having'
донистан 'to know'	**доно** 'wise'
расидан 'to reach (maturity)'	**расо** 'mature, exact'
дидан 'to see'	**бино** 'capable of seeing'
гуфтан 'to say'	**гӯё** 'capable of speech'
гирифтан 'to get'	**гиро** 'attractive'
шунидан 'to hear'	**шунаво** 'capable of hearing'

5.2. Finite verb forms: The indicative active tenses

a. Simple past tense. The simple past tense of all verbs is formed by adding the past tense endings to the past stem of the verb. The past tense endings are:

	Sing.	*Plur.*
1st	**-ам**	**-ем**
2nd	**-й**	**-ед**
3rd	**-ø**	**-анд**

The past stem (identical with the 3rd person singular form) is formed from the infinitive by dropping the final **-ан**; because all past stems end in the consonants **д** or **т**, there is never need to worry about changing vowels in the endings into yoted letters in the simple past tense. The stress falls on the first syllable of the verb. In colloquial speech, the 3rd person plural ending **-анд** is pronounced **-ан**; because the stress is on the first syllable, this is pronounced differently than the infinitive. Thus, the past tense stem of **хӯрдан** 'to do' is **хӯрд**, and its simple past tense forms are as follows.

	Singular	Plural
1ˢᵗ	хӯрдам, 'I ate'	хӯрдем, 'we ate'
2ⁿᵈ	хӯрдӣ, 'you (*sg.*) ate'	хӯрдед, 'you (*pl.*) ate'
3ʳᵈ	хӯрд, 'he/she/it ate'	хӯрданд, 'they ate'

Ман гул харидам, 'I bought a flower.'
Онҳо шӯрбо пухтанд, 'They cooked some soup.'
Мо ба Париж рафтем, 'We went to Paris.'

The simple past tense is used for actions that happened or conditions that ended at a definite time in the past, with no further qualifications. It corresponds closely to the English simple past in meaning. It is not used for statements about actions that were habitual or ongoing in the past, such as "I went to the store every Friday" or "I read that book while you were here." (These sentences use the simple past in English but can be rewritten with other past tense forms that correspond to the tenses used in Tajiki: "I would go/used to go to the store every Friday" and "I was reading that book while you were here.") It is also not used for actions that occurred at some indefinite point in the past (what is called the "experiential past"), such as "I've read that book" (the time when I read it doesn't matter and isn't specified, only the fact that I have read it—that I have had the experience of reading it), "I haven't gone there before" (where the focus is on the fact that I've never been there at any time in the past), "I've been there once or twice," (the important point is that at one or two unspecified times in the past I had gone there) or "Have you ever gone to France?" (in which the entire point of the question is whether at any time in the past I have been in France). These sentences do not use the simple past, but other sentences of the same type can take the simple past in English: "Yeah, I read that book" (which can be either simple past or experiential past, depending on context), "I never went there when I lived in Chicago," and "Did you ever go to France?," for example. (As a rule of thumb, if the sentence includes adverbs like "ever," "never," "always," "often," "before," "once," "twice," or "a few times," the sentence does not refer to a definite time in the past and the simple past cannot be used in Tajiki.) In short, the simple past tense refers to some specific time in the past; if the sentence has any other implication, other past tense forms are used.

In addition, in colloquial Tajiki the simple past tense is used for emphasis for events that are going to occur very soon. Thus, the usual meaning of **Чӣ гуфтед?** is "What did you say?," but it can also be used in speaking to mean, "What is your opinion?" (that is, "What do/will you say?"). Similarly, **рафтем** ordinarily means "We went," but used emphatically can mean, "Let's go!" (a meaning usually expressed with the present subjunctive form **равем**, which is not as emphatic).

The negative of the past tense forms is formed by adding the prefix **на-** to the simple past tense form; **на-** always takes the stress. It corresponds to the English past negative formed with *didn't* — that is, it expresses the simple negative without any other connotations; it does not express such meanings as 'I haven't read this book (yet).' Negative sentences are formed exactly like the corresponding positive sentences:

Ман нахӯрдам, 'I didn't eat.'
Ту ба хона нарафтӣ, 'You didn't go home.'
Вай муаллимро надид, 'She didn't see the teacher.'

Yes/no questions are formed from the corresponding simple statements by changing the intonation:

Шумо шароб нӯшидед?   'Did you drink some wine?'
Ту ба хона нарафтӣ?   'Didn't you go home?'
Вай муаллимро надид?   'She didn't see the teacher?'

b. Present continuous tense. The present continuous tense indicates an action that is ongoing or in progress at the present time; that is, it is used for actions that at the time of speaking have begun but are not yet completed. It corresponds closely in meaning to the English present progressive but can only be used with action verbs, not with verbs like **доштан** 'to have' that indicate an unchanging state. It is a compound tense formed from the past participle of the main verb, the past participle **истода** of the auxiliary **истодан** 'to stand,' and the predicate endings. For example, the written forms of the present continuous of the verb **хӯрдан** 'to eat' are:

For example:

	Singular	Plural
1st	хӯрда истодаам 'I am eating'	хӯрда истодаем 'we are eating'
2nd	хӯрда истодай 'you (sg.) are eating'	хӯрда истодаед 'you (pl.) are eating'
3rd	хӯрда истодааст 'he/she/it is eating'	хӯрда истодаанд 'they are eating'

Ман ба апаам мактуб навишта истодаам,
'I am writing a letter to my older sister.'
Вай кор карда истодааст, 'He is working.'
Онҳо дар боғ сайругашт карда истодаанд,
'They are strolling in the garden.'
Шумо чӣ кор карда истодаед? 'What are you doing?'

However, the pronunciation differs from the spelling (which is purely historical). In the northern dialect these forms are pronounced: In the southern dialect, on the other hand, they are pronounced:

	Singular	Plural
1st	хӯрдосам 'I am eating'	хӯрдосем 'we are eating'
2nd	хӯрдосӣ 'you (sg.) are eating'	хӯрдосед 'you (pl.) are eating'
3rd	хӯрдос 'he/she/it is eating'	хӯрдосан 'they are eating'

The negative is formed by adding the negative prefix **на-** to the main verb; yes/no questions are shown by intonation.

	Singular	Plural
1st	хурдестам 'I am eating'	хурдестем 'we are eating'
2nd	хурдестӣ 'you (sg.) are eating'	хурдестед 'you (pl.) are eating'
3rd	хурдестай 'he/she/it is eating'	хурдестан 'they are eating'

Ман ҳеҷ кор накарда истодаам, 'I'm not doing anything.'
Вай кор накарда истодааст, 'She isn't working.'
Шумо вазифаи хонагиатонро накарда истодаед?
'Aren't you doing your homework?'

Because the present continuous tense indicates an ongoing action, it requires a definite time reference, often an adverb like **ҳоло** 'now' or **ҳозир** 'now.'

c. Past continuous tense. The past continuous tense is used to indicate that an action was ongoing at a particular time in the past: *When you called I was reading a book.* That is, it is the past-time equivalent of the present continuous tense. It is formed in the same way as the present continuous tense, except that the predicate endings are replaced by the simple past of **будан** 'to be':

	Singular	Plural
1st	хӯрда истода будам 'I was eating'	хӯрда истода будем 'we were eating'
2nd	хӯрда истода будӣ 'you (sg.) were eating'	хӯрда истода будед 'you (pl.) were eating'
3rd	хӯрда истода буд 'he/she/it was eating'	хӯрда истода буданд 'they were eating'

Ман ба апаам мактуб навишта истода будам,
'I was writing a letter to my older sister.'
Вай кор карда истода буд, 'He was working.'
Онҳо дар боғ сайругашт карда истода буданд,
'They were strolling in the garden.'
Шумо чӣ кор карда истода будед? 'What were you doing?'

As with the present continuous tense, the pronunciation is different from the spelling. In the northern dialect these forms are pronounced **кардоса будам** 'I was doing,' etc., while in the southern dialect they are pronounced **кардеста будам** 'I was doing,' etc.

Just as with the present continuous tense, the negative is formed by prefixing **на-** to the main verb; yes/no questions are indicated by intonation; and the past continuous tense can only be used with action verbs.

Ман ҳеҷ кор накарда истода будам, 'I wasn't doing anything.'
Вай кор накарда истода буд, 'She wasn't working.'
Шумо вазифаи хонагиатонро накарда истода будед?
'Weren't you doing your homework?'

The past continuous tense can be used by itself if the time in the past when the action was taking place is clear from context. However, it usually requires an explicit time reference, and thus is often used to indicate the background to a past action that is more important to the conversation, such as a past time marker or a subordinate clause of past time.

> **Вақте ки ман ба хона омадам, занам хӯрок пухта истода буд,**
> 'When I came home, my wife was cooking dinner.'
> **Дирӯз ман ба кор рафта истода будам, ки дар роҳ Додоро дидам,**
> 'Yesterday, I was going to work when I saw Dodo in the street.'
> **Мо дарс хонда истода будем, ки аз берун овози гиряи кӯдак ба гӯш расид,**
> 'We were studying the lesson when we heard the sound of a child crying outside.'

d. Present-future tense. This tense is used to indicate an action that is either ongoing or habitual in the present or that will occur in the future. It is formed by adding the present-future tense endings (which are identical to the past tense endings except the 3rd singular ending **-ад**) and the prefix **ме-** to the present stem of the verb. The verb **хондан/хон** 'to read' is conjugated in the present-future tense as follows:

	Singular	Plural
1st	**мехонам** 'I read'	**мехонем** 'we read'
2nd	**мехонӣ** 'you (sg.) read'	**мехонед** 'you (pl.) read'
3rd	**мехонад** 'he/she/it reads'	**мехонанд** 'they read'

In compound verbs, **ме-** follows the nominal complement, which is written as a separate word: **дӯст медорам** 'I like,' **кор мекунад** 'he works,' and so on. In prefixed verbs **ме-** usually precedes the prefix, but with separable prefixes **ме-** immediately precedes the verb and the prefix is written joined to it: **вомехӯрем** 'we meet' (from **вохӯрдан** 'to meet'). The stress falls on the first syllable, **ме-** for simple verbs and the prefix or nominal part otherwise.

The negative is formed by prefixing **на-** immediately before **ме-**; it takes the stress. As with the positive forms, nominal complements are written as separate words and separable prefixes are joined to the rest of the verb: **кор намекунад** 'he doesn't work,' **вонамехӯрем** 'we don't/won't meet.'

The prefix **ме-** indicates ongoing or continuing action, as in the past continuous tense; historically it was not added to stative verbs, that is, verbs indicating an ongoing state. However, in the present-future tense it is now used with all verbs except **доштан** (when used as a simple verb in the meaning 'to have'); moreover, **ме-** *is* used with **доштан** in the present-future tense when it is part of a compound verb or when it is used in the meaning 'to hold': **Ман биринҷ дӯст медорам,** 'I like rice.'

More specifically, the present-future tense is used:

1) For habitual actions in the present; that is, actions that happened regularly in the past (for however long a time) and continue to happen regularly in the present and into the future. In this sense it often translates the English simple present, which in fact for most action verbs has a habitual sense: "I work" (every day, say) as opposed to "I am working" (right now).

2) For continuous actions in the present or future, like the present continuous, only with less emphasis upon the continuity of the action.

3) In narration about the past to give a vivid character to the story; colloquial English has a similar usage: "So yesterday I go in this store, see, and the owner asks me…"

e. Past imperfect(habitual) tense. The past imperfect tense is used to indicate actions that were habitual or occupational or that happened regularly in the past, such as *When I was a child, I would read a book every week* or *He went to school when he lived in Panjakent*; it can be translated 'used to do,' 'would do,' or 'did' depending on context. It is formed by adding the prefix **ме-** to the appropriate form of the simple past:

	Singular	Plural
1st	**мехондам** 'I used to read'	**мехондем** 'we used to read'
2nd	**мехондӣ** 'you (*sg.*) used to read'	**мехондед** 'you (*pl.*) used to read'
3rd	**мехонд** 'he/she/it used to read'	**мехонданд** 'they used to read'

Соли гузашта ман ҳар ҳафта ба бародарам мактуб менавиштам,
'Last year I used to write letters to my brother every week.'
Солҳои донишҷӯйй мо бисёр китоб мехондем,
'We used to read lots of books when we were students.'
Он солҳо мо дар Токио зиндагӣ мекардем,
'In those days (during those years), we lived in Tokyo.'
Падарам дар донишгоҳ кор мекард,
'My father worked (used to work) in a university.'

The past imperfect cannot be used to refer to a definite time in the past, but instead must refer to a period of time within which the action used to occur. Nor can the past imperfect be used for a definite, delimited period of time (*for three months*, for example). If a definite time or duration or a single action is indicated, the simple past must be used. (On the other hand, an indication of *frequency* is perfectly acceptable with the past imperfect, such as **ҳар ҳафта** 'each week.') That is, the past imperfect focuses upon the habitual or ongoing character of the action, while the simple past implies a completed action in the past and is used to focus on the circumstances around it.

Дирӯз ман ба Эдвард мактуб навиштам,
'Yesterday I wrote a letter to Edward.' (*There is reference to a definite time during which a single action occurred, writing a letter, hence the simple past.*)
Вақте ки ман дар Испания будам, ҳар ҳафта ба Эдвард мактуб менавиштам, 'When I was in Spain, I used to write letters to Edward every week.' (*There is reference to an extended period during which the action occurred repeatedly and habitually, hence the past imperfect.*)
Мо панҷ сол дар Канада зиндагӣ кардем,
'We lived in Canada for five years.' (*The condition of living in Canada extended throughout a definite period, hence the simple past.*)
Солҳои ҳафтодум мо дар Канада зиндагӣ мекардем,
'In the seventies, we lived in Canada.' (*The condition of living in Canada only occurred at some unspecified period during the seventies, hence the past imperfect.*)

For this reason, the past imperfect is often used when describing a past situation as the background to another action at a definite time in the past.

Вақте ки хоҳарам таваллуд шуд, падарам дар донишгоҳ кормекард, 'When my younger sister was born, my father was working at the university.'

Stative verbs like **будан** 'to be' and **доштан** 'to have' do not take the prefix **ме-** (except in certain conditional sentences). That is, only active verbs have a distinct past imperfect tense.

Модарам хонашинзан буд,
'My mother was a housewife' (not ***мебуд).

f. Present perfect tense. The present perfect is formed by adding the predicate endings to the past participle. Note that (1) the 3rd singular **аст** is written joined to the participle, and (2) although a **й** is sometimes added between the participle and the predicate endings, it is not indicated in writing with yoted letters (thus, **хондаам** can be pronounced [хондаям]):

	Singular	Plural
1st	**хондаам** 'I have read'	**хондаем** 'we have read'
2nd	**хондай** 'you (*sg.*) have read'	**хондаед** 'you (*pl.*) have read'
3rd	**хондааст** 'he/she/it has read'	**хондаанд** 'they have read'

The negative is formed using the appropriate form of the past participle; **на-** takes primary stress and the last syllable of the participle takes secondary stress (as does the noun of a compound verb): **нарафтаам** 'I haven't gone,' **вонахӯрдаем** 'we haven't met.'

The present perfect has two distinct uses.
1) The present perfect proper is used to indicate an action that was completed at some time in the past but whose end result continues into the present; in this use it corresponds to the English present perfect: *I have eaten, he's gone,* etc.

Парвиз бисёр шароб нӯшидааст,
'Parviz has drunk a lot of wine.'
Назокат аз Фаронса омадааст,
'Nazokat has come from France.'
Онҳо ба Карочӣ рафтаанд, 'They have gone to Karachi.'

The present perfect expresses an action the result of which is clear. When this tense is used in this meaning, sometimes it is preceded by explanatory phrases like **маълум аст** 'it is clear,' **маълум шуд** 'it became clear,' and **маълум мешавад** 'it is/becomes clear.' Narrative tenses used without these phrases are logically results of such explanations.

Example:
Маълум шуд, ки ӯро ҳабс кардаанд,
'It was clear that they arrested him.'
Ана фаҳмидед, ӯ наомадааст,
'Well then, you understood that he hasn't come.'

The present perfect is also used as in English to indicate the "experiential past," that is, that an action has (or has not) occurred at some time in the past.

Шумо ба Париж рафтаед? 'Have you (ever) gone to Paris?'
Ман бузкаширо тамошо накардаам,
'I've never watched buzkashi *(a game in which several horsemen compete to capture the body of a dead goat)*.'
Ман борҳо ба Тошканд рафтаам,
'I've been to Tashkent several times.'
Саврӣ филмҳои амрикойиро бисёр дидааст,
'Savri has seen a lot of American films.'
Падарам ҳеҷ гоҳ маро ҷанг накардааст,
'My father has never argued with me.'

In English you can distinguish these senses of the present perfect with certain adverbs: The experiential past takes *before* in a positive statement, *ever (before)* in a simple question, and *never* in a negative statement or question; the present perfect proper takes *already* in a positive statement and *yet* in a negative statement or a question. To specify that the present perfect is meant rather than the experiential past, Tajiki uses the adverbs **ҳанӯз** 'yet,' **то ҳол** 'so far, until now,' and **аллакай** 'already.'

То ҳол се бор ба ӯ занг задаам,
'So far, I have called her three times.'

Note: *Neither the present perfect nor the experiential past can be used to speak of a definite time in the past; they refer to actions occurring at some* *indefinite point within an extended period of time. Therefore, a past time marker requires the simple past (or another past tense referring to a definite time in the past), except when using the reportative past (see next).*

2) The present perfect is also used as the reportative or narrative past, that is, to indicate that the statement is based on hearsay or the testimony of others, not on first-hand knowledge of the speaker. This use is very common for passing on common knowledge, reporting what experts say, and telling about the historical past.

Говхо ба он водӣ набаромадаанд,
'Cows don't go into that valley.'
Мувофиқи гуфти онҳо, ӯ бо модараш ба Юнон рафтааст,
'According to what they say (their words), he went to Greece with his mother.'

When used as the reportative past, the present perfect can be used with a past time marker.

Дар вақти вафоти падарам ман ёздаҳмоҳа будаам,
'I was eleven months old at the time of my father's death.'
Note: *The reportative form must be used because this information must have been learned from others.*
Исмоили Сомонӣ дар соли 907 мурдааст,
'Ismoil Somoni died in 907 AD.'

g. Past distant tense. The past distant tense is formed in much the same way as the present perfect, with the past tense of **будан** in place of the predicate endings:

	Singular	Plural
1st	дида будам 'I had seen'	дида будем 'we had seen'
2nd	дида будӣ 'you (sg.) had seen'	дида будед 'you (pl.) had seen'
3rd	дида буд 'he/she/it had seen'	дида буданд 'they had seen'

As its name suggests, the past distant is used to tell about events in the relatively distant past.

Зулфия дар соли 1997 ба Амрико омада буд,
'Zulfia came to America in 1997.'

Бори аввал ман тобистони соли 1995 ба Лондон рафта будам,
'I went to London the first time in the summer of 1995.'
Ман се сол пеш ба Тоҷикистон сафар карда будам,
'I traveled to Tajikistan three years ago.'

The past distant is also used as the past perfect (*he had gone*), to indicate an action that was already completed but with continuing consequences at a given time in the past:

Соли гузашта ӯ аллакай рисолаашро дифоъ карда буд,
'Last year he'd already defended his thesis.'
Вақте ки ман ӯро дидам, ӯ аллакай аз Лондон баргашта буд,
'When I saw him, he had already returned from London.'

h. Future tense forms. There are two verb forms to express the future in Tajiki. The future participle is common in colloquial Tajiki; the simple future is more literary.

1. Future participle: The future participle is used in colloquial Tajiki as a future tense indicating that an action is intended, planned, desired, or hoped for. It is used like a predicate adjective to which the predicate endings are added (except in the 2nd person singular, in which the repetition of **-ӣ** is felt to be redundant):

Ман ба Париж рафтаниям,
'I want to go to Paris, I plan to go to Paris.'
Ту соли оянда ба Масков рафтанӣ?
'Do you plan to go to Moscow next year?'

It can also be used in other tenses, such as the past and the present perfect, to indicate the appropriate sense of intention in the past:

Ман ба Париж рафтанӣ будам,
'I wanted to go to Paris, I planned to go to Paris.'

2. Simple (or literary) future: The simple future tense is used exclusively for actions that will occur in the future. It is formed from the present subjunctive (see Section 5.3b below) of **хостан** 'to want' immediately followed by the past stem of the verb; when used in this way as an auxiliary for the future tense, the verb **хостан** loses its original meaning of 'to want' and merely conveys information about the person and number of the subject of the sentence.

	Singular	Plural
1st	хоҳам кард 'I will do'	хоҳем кард 'we will do'
2nd	хоҳӣ кард 'you (sg.) will do'	хоҳед кард 'you (pl.) will do'
3rd	хоҳад кард 'he/she/it will do'	хоҳанд кард 'they will do'

Ҳафтаи оянда ман ба Душанбе хоҳам рафт,
'Next week I will go to Dushanbe.'
Ман ба Маскав хоҳам рафт,
'I will go to Moscow.'
Фирӯз баъд аз се рӯз хоҳад омад,
'Firuz will come after three days.'

The negative is formed by adding **на-** to **хоҳ-**.

Мо оид ба он нахоҳем гуфт, 'We won't talk about it again.'
Ман нахоҳам рафт, 'I will not go.'
Ту нахоҳӣ гуфт, 'You will not say.'

The simple future is largely a literary tense; in spoken Tajiki the future participle or the present-future tense is usually used in its place.

5.3. The other finite verb forms

a. **Imperative**. The imperative is used to give commands; for almost all verbs it is formed with the present stem. In the singular, the bare present stem is used; in the plural, the suffix **-ед** is added:

Ин китобро хонед! 'Read this book!'
Инро гир! 'Take this!'

The imperative of **будан** is formed with **бош**:

Тайёр бош! 'Be prepared!'
(*the Boy Scout motto in Tajiki*)
Зинда бош, эй Ватан, / Тоҷикистони озоди ман!
'Live long, O Motherland, My free Tajikistan!'

(the refrain from the national anthem, **Суруди Миллӣ**)
Саломат бошед! 'Be healthy!' (*as farewell*), 'You're welcome!'

The verb **додан/диҳ** 'to give' changes **диҳ** to **деҳ** in the singular to form the imperative: **Ба ман онро деҳ!** 'Give that to me!', but remains as **диҳед** in plural form: **Китобро диҳед!** 'Give the book!' In colloquial Tajiki, **деҳ** and **диҳед** 'give!' are pronounced **те** and **тед**: **Косая/Косара те!** 'Give (me) the bowl!'

Many verbs whose present stems are very short add the prefix **би-** to form the imperative; a **й** is automatically added before a vowel, so the imperative of **омадан/о** 'to come' is frequently written **биё(ед)**, and the imperative of **овардан/овар** (whose present stem **овар** often contracts to **ор**) 'to bring' is often **биёр(ед)**.

In older Persian **би-** often indicated the subjunctive (as it still does in Iran); this use can be encountered in poetry and song.

b. Present subjunctive. The subjunctive is used to express uncertainty about the completion of an action or to deny the current existence of a state, including expressions of possibility, probability, desire, intent, doubt, and the like. The present subjunctive of most verbs is formed by adding the present personal endings to the present stem of the verb. In other words, for almost all verbs the subjunctive has the same form as the present indicative without the prefix **ме-**.

	Singular	Plural
1st	хонам 'that I read'	хонем 'that we read'
2nd	хонӣ 'that you (sg.) read'	хонед 'that you (pl.) read'
3rd	хонад 'that he/she/it read'	хонанд 'that they read'

The verbs **будан** 'to be' and **доштан** 'to have' form the subjunctive differently. The subjunctive of **будан** is formed with the stem **бош**:

	Singular	Plural
1st	бошам 'that I be'	бошем 'that we be'
2nd	бошӣ 'that you (sg.) be'	бошед 'that you (pl.) be'
3rd	бошад 'that he/she/it be'	бошанд 'that they be'

Шод бошанд, 'May they be happy.'

There is an alternate form of the 3rd singular, **бод**:

Зинда бод!	'Long may he/it live!'
Поянда бод!	'Forever live…!'
Хуҷаста бод!	'Let him be happy!'
Нест/нобуд бод!	'Let him be gone, down with…!'

Because **доштан** does not take **ме-** in the present indicative, to prevent ambiguity its subjunctive is formed from the past participle **дошта** and the auxiliary stem **бош**:

	Singular	Plural
1st	**дошта бошам** 'that I have'	**дошта бошем** 'that we have'
2nd	**дошта боши** 'that you (sg.) have'	**дошта бошед** 'that you (pl.) have'
3rd	**дошта бошад** 'that he/she/it have'	**дошта бошанд** 'that they have'

Note that this form is used for the present subjunctive of compound verbs in **доштан** as well: **дӯст дошта бошам** 'that I like.'

The plural imperative of all verbs except **доштан** and **додан** is identical in form with the 2nd person plural of the present subjunctive; thus, **бошед** can mean either 'be!' or 'may you be' depending on context.

The subjunctive is almost non-existent in English, so its use can be hard for English speakers to grasp. The essential use of the subjunctive is to indicate that an action is not actual but rather potential, projected, expected, desired, necessary, possible, or contingent on another action. Thus, in most cases the use of the subjunctive is required by the use of other words, such as modal verbs (*can, should, might, ought,* etc.) and some conjunctions (*if, lest, before,* etc.), or by particular constructions (certain types of relative clauses, conditional statements, etc.). In these uses the verb in the subjunctive does not stand alone but is in some way connected loosely but in a dependent sense to another verb (sometimes one that is omitted but understood) in the same sentence.

However, the subjunctive can be used alone to indicate a strong wish. For the 1st person singular and plural, the subjunctive means "let me…" or "I shall…" and "let's…", respectively, while for other persons it is best translated "may…" (or "let him…" or "let them…").

Бинам.	'Let me see, I shall see.'
Равем!	'Let's go!'
Саломат бошад!	'May he be healthy!'
Саломат бошед!	'May you be healthy!'

In addition, the subjunctive can be used in parallel clauses to indicate a general truth (a "gnomic statement") or to equate two or more actions without subordinating any of them. This use is quite common in proverbs:

Забон донӣ, ҷаҳон донӣ, 'Learn a language, learn a world.'

Note that this construction pictures the two actions as perfectly parallel and as true regardless of circumstances. It would be possible to make it a true conditional statement by adding **агар** 'if' to the beginning, but doing so would imply that learning a language is a means to learning a world and would set up an ordering of before and after that the use of subjunctives in parallel avoids, which instead implies that as you learn a language, so also and as a matter of course you learn a world (a connotation the English equivalent conveys somewhat as well).

c. Other subjunctives. Besides the present subjunctive, there are three compound subjunctive forms, the perfect, habitual, and continuous subjunctives, differing from the present subjunctive in aspect and finding use largely in conditional sentences (see Chapter 5, Section 7). The translations given emphasize the distinction each form makes, but they would often be too clumsy to use in English; in general they are much rarer than the present subjunctive and the learner should only learn how to recognize them at this stage.

кунам, 'that I do'
карда бошам, 'that I (would) have done'
мекарда бошам, 'that I would usually do'
карда истода бошам, 'that I would be doing'

Агар ман ин корро намекарда бошам, ҳолам вазнин мешавад, 'If I didn't have this job, I'd be in bad shape (my condition would be serious).' **Note:** *The habitual subjunctive is used to mean working at a job rather than doing a particular piece of work.*
Агар ман туро дида бошам, чаро дар хотир надорам? 'If I had seen you, why don't I remember?'
Note: *The continual subjunctive is used to emphasize that the speaker's seeing the hearer was ongoing when the hearer noticed it.*

d. **Passive voice**. The passive is a verb form used to make the logical object of a verb (the person or thing actually being acted on) into the subject. Thus, the active sentence *I saw Bill* has the passive equivalent *Bill was seen by me*. The passive is used to focus attention on the logical object (the patient) rather than or without mentioning the logical subject (the agent): *Bill was seen entering the house*. The main way to form the passive in Tajiki is from the past participle of the verb in the active sentence and the auxiliary **шудан**, which shows the tense. For example, **хондан** 'to read' has the passive **хонда шудан** 'to be read,' which is conjugated normally:

Active		Passive
гирифтан 'to take'	>	гирифта шудан 'to be taken'
сохтан 'to build'	>	сохта шудан 'to be built'
куштан 'to kill'	>	кушта шудан 'to be killed'

Онҳо китобро хонданд, 'They read the book.'
• Китоб хонда шуд, 'The book was read.'
Онҳо китобро мехонанд, 'They read the book.'
• Китоб хонда мешавад, 'The book is being/is/will be read.'
Онҳо китобро хондаанд, 'They have read the book.'
• Китоб хонда шудааст, 'The book has been read.'

Similarly:
Ман хона сохтам, 'I built a house.'
• Хона сохта шуд, 'The house was built.'
Ман хона месозам, 'I am going to build a house.'
• Хона сохта мешавад, 'The house is going to be built.'

However, compound verbs form the passive in a second way. For most auxiliary verbs used in active compound verbs, there is a corresponding passive auxiliary; for the most common active auxiliary, **кардан**, its passive auxiliary is **шудан**, for example. The passive of the compound verb is formed simply by replacing the active auxiliary with its corresponding passive; for example, **тамом кардан** 'to finish (*something*)' has the passive **тамом шудан** 'to be finished.' Compound nominative verbs formed with the auxiliary verbs **шудан**, **гаштан/гард** 'to turn (*intr*.),' **гардидан/гард** 'to wander,' **ёфтан/ёб** 'to find' and **дидан/бин** 'to see, meet with' are always passive.

Active	Passive
гарм кардан 'to warm up (*trans.*)'	> **гарм шудан** 'to become warm'
об кардан 'to melt (*trans.*)'	> **об шудан** 'to melt (*intr.*)'
қуфл кардан 'to lock'	> **қуфл шудан** 'to be locked'
сар кардан 'to start, begin (*trans.*)'	> **сар шудан** 'to be started, begin(*intr.*)'

Модарам об гарм кард, 'My mother heated the water.'
• **Оби чойник гарм шуд,** 'The water in the kettle became hot.'
Модарам об гарм мекунад, 'My mother is heating the water.'
• **Оби чойник гарм мешавад,** 'The water in the kettle is heating up.'
Пахта ҷамъ гардид, 'The cotton was gathered.'
• **Об ҷамъ гашт,** 'The water was collected.'
Мусофирон зарар диданд,
'The passengers were injured (suffered harm).'
Кор поён ёфт, 'The work was finished (came to an end).'

The logical subject of the sentence (the agent) is indicated with the phrase **аз тарафи** 'by' (literally, "from the side of"):

Ман аз тарафи ҳукумати Амрико ба Вашингтон даъват шудам,
'I was invited to Washington by the American government.'
Китоб аз тарафи Дилбар хонда шуд,
'The book was read by Dilbar.'

Tajiki uses the passive less frequently and more strictly than English does. In English, it is possible to form passive sentences in which the indirect object or another part of speech is made the subject. For example, *I gave Mary the book* can have both *The book was given to Mary* (true passive) and *Mary was given the book* (passive of the indirect object) as passives, at least for many speakers of English. Similarly, it is natural for some English speakers to make passives for objects of prepositions: *They went through the house thoroughly* (active) and *The house was gone through thoroughly* (passive). Tajiki only allows true passives, in which a direct object is made the subject; **Китоб ба Дилбар дода шуд,** 'The book was given to Dilbar' is grammatical but *****Дилбар китобро дода шуд,** 'Dilbar was given the book' is ungrammatical. Moreover, Tajiki tends not to use the passive when the agent is specified, and when the subject is general or unspecified Tajiki tends to use an impersonal construction or a 3rd person plural active form. Since the purpose of the passive is to focus attention on the direct object, this emphasis can often be shown in Tajiki simply by moving the direct object to the beginning of the sentence.

e. Causative voice. The causative indicates that the subject makes someone do something or causes something to happen. It is formed by adding the suffix **-он** to the present stem of the verb; the past stem of the causative is then formed in the usual fashion with **-ид** or **-д**. Thus, from **хондан** 'to read,' present stem **хон**, the present stem **хонон** of the causative and its infinitive **хонондан** 'to make someone read' are formed. Similarly, from **нишастан/шин** 'to sit' is formed the causative **шинондан/шинон** 'to cause to sit, to have someone sit, to seat; to place, to plant.' The causative often takes an idiomatic meaning, as with the many meanings of **шинондан**. (Whether the past stem ends in **-ид** or **-д** must be learned for each verb. Some verbs have both forms, usually with no difference in meaning: **гардон(и)дан** 'to turn around, return (*trans.*); to hand back.' In a few cases the two stems have different meanings: **гузарондан** 'to pass (*trans.*), spend (*time*)' vs. **гузаронидан** 'to celebrate.')

The grammar associated with the causative varies depending on the type of verb it is. If the active verb is *intransitive*, then the subject of the active verb (the person or thing being caused to act in the causative) is made the direct object of the causative verb, just as in English.

> **Вай ба хонааш давид,** 'He ran home.'
> • **Ман вайро ба хонааш давондам,** 'I made him run home.'
> **Мо нишастем,** 'We sat down.'
> • **Далер моро шинонд,** 'Daler seated us.'

If the active verb is *transitive*, however, the subject of the active verb is made the indirect object of the causative verb; the direct object of the active verb remains the direct object of the causative verb as well. Because the subject of the active verb is made into an indirect object, it is possible to indicate it with the object suffix on the causative verb.

> **Ман китобро хондам,** 'I read the book.'
> • **Падарам ба ман китобро хонондand,**
> 'My father made me read the book.'
> • **Падарам китобро хонондандам,**
> 'My father made me read the book.'

Парвиз палов хӯрд, 'Parviz ate pilaf.'
• **Мо ба Парвиз палов хӯрондем,**
'We made Parviz eat pilaf; we fed Parviz pilaf.'

The passive of a causative (*He was made to run*) is formed in the usual way. It indicates that the subject was forced to do something or brought into a given state by someone else.

Он дарахт панҷ сол пеш шинонда шудааст,
'That tree was planted five years ago.'

f. Reportative forms. As mentioned previously, the present perfect is also used as a reportative tense form indicating information obtained at second hand (by hearsay, reputation, or report, for example). Since it is reporting something already observed, the verb indicates past time. However, there are three other reportative tense forms differing from the simple reportative (present perfect) in the *aspect* of the verb. The simple reportative form indicates both perfective and imperfective aspect (though it is not used in all cases of perfective aspect), and is by far the most commonly-used form; the others are much rarer and the learner only needs to recognize them at this stage.

The reportative habitual (or past habitual narrative) is formed from the simple reportative by adding the prefix **ме-**. It is used to indicate a statement at second hand for all actions that are habitual or repeated.

Мардҳо дар ҷангҳо ва занҳо ҳангоми таваллуд вафот мекардаанд, 'Men die in battle and women die in childbirth.' **Note:** *The use of the reportative habitual implies that this is a statement about typical, regular occurrences.*
Мардҳо нисбат ба занҳо бисёртар сигор мекашидаанд,
'Men smoke more compared to women.'
Шумо дар Лондон зиндагӣ мекардаед,
'(I hear) you used to live in London.'

The reportative past distant tense is used to indicate a statement at second hand in the same circumstances the simple past distant would be used—to tell about events in the relatively distant past, and actions that had been completed at a certain point in the past with continuing consequences. It is formed by combining

the past participle with the simple reportative (present perfect) of
будан: **дида будаам, дида будай, дида будааст**, etc.

> **Ӯ ба бародараш занг назада будааст,**
> 'He didn't fight/hadn't fought with his brother.'
> **Комрон ӯро дар куҷо дида будааст?**
> 'Where did Komron see him?'
> **Ман то он рӯз муаллими бачаҳоямро надида будаам,**
> 'Until that day I had not seen my teacher's children.'
> **Пеш аз омадани Шумо бародарам ҳанӯз ба мактаб нарафта будааст,**
> 'Before you came my brother hadn't yet gone to school.'
> **Ӯ пеш аз ман ба ин ҷо расида будааст,**
> 'He (had) arrived here before I did.'

Finally, the reportative continuous tense indicates continuous aspect, and thus that the action was reported as ongoing in the past. It is formed by using the simple reportative of **будан** in the construction for the present and past continuous: **рафта истода будааст**, 'he/she was going,' etc.

> **Вақте ки вай пулро ёфт, вай китобашро кофта истода будааст,**
> '(They say) she was looking for her book when she found the money.'

6. Modal verbs

Auxiliary verbs and verbal forms are widely used in Tajiki and can be divided into two types, modal verbs and auxiliary verbs proper (see Chapter 5, Section 3); in general modal verbs have the same subject as the main verb and auxiliaries do not. There are four modal verbs or verbal constructions in Tajiki, indicating ability (*can*), desire (*want/wish*), necessity (*must*), and possibility (*might*) with a wide variety of shades of meaning depending on tense.

The verbs **хостан** 'to want' and **тавонистан** 'to be able, can' are used with a main verb occurring either in a non-finite form or in the subjunctive. First the non-finite constructions will be given, then the subjunctive construction.

a. Expression of ability. To say that a person is able (**тавонистан**) to do something (main verb), the main verb is put in the past participle, which must immediately precede **тавонистан/тавон**, which is conjugated; thus, in the present-future tense:

	Singular	Plural
1st	**ман...дида метавонам** 'I can see'	**мо...дида метавонем** 'we can see'
2nd	**ту...дида метавонӣ** 'you (*sg.*) can see'	**шумо...дида метавонед** 'you (*pl.*) can see'
3rd	**ӯ...дида метавонад** 'he can see'	**онҳо...дида метавонанд** 'they can see'

Both the auxiliary and the main verb may be negated. The meaning follows from the simple combination of the two verbs; thus, if the main verb is negated, the sentence indicates refraining from that action, and if **тавонистан** is negated, it indicates an inability to do the action.

Ман нигоҳ карда наметавонам, 'I am not able to look.'
Ман нигоҳ накарда метавонам,
'I am able to refrain from looking.'
Ман нигоҳ накарда наметавонам,
'I am not able to refrain from looking.'

Other tenses can be formed by conjugating **тавонистан** in the appropriate tense. Note that **тавонистан** is a stative verb, not an active verb, so it cannot take the present or past continuous tenses.

Имрӯз ман вайро дида тавонистаниям,
'I will be able to see him today.'
Ман дида натавонистам, 'I was not able to see.'
Ман надида тавонистам, 'I was able to refrain from seeing'
Ман надида натавонистам,
'I was not able to refrain from seeing.'

In the subjunctive construction, ability is expressed by conjugating the present of the subjunctive auxiliary **тавонистан** 'to be able' immediately after the subject. Thus, if the main verb is **хӯрдан** 'to eat, to drink,' the conjugation appears as follows:

	Singular	Plural
1st	метавонам...хӯрам 'I can eat'	метавонем...хӯрем 'we can eat'
2nd	метавонӣ...хӯрӣ 'you (sg.) can eat'	метавонед...хӯред 'you (pl.) can eat'
3rd	метавонад...хӯрад 'he can eat'	метавонанд...хӯранд 'they can eat'

As with the non-finite construction, the auxiliary and the main verb may be negated:

> Ман наметавонам бинам, 'I am not able to see.'
> Ман метавонам набинам, 'I am able to refrain from seeing'
> Ман наметавонам набинам, 'I am not able to refrain from seeing.'

Other tenses can be formed by conjugating **тавонистан** in the appropriate tense.

> Ман тавонистам бинам, 'I was able to see him today.'
> Ман натавонистам бинам, 'I was not able to see.'
> Ман тавонистам набинам, 'I was able to refrain from seeing'
> Ман натавонистам набинам, 'I was not able to refrain from seeing.'

b. Expression of desire. Desire is expressed by the infinitive of the main verb followed the appropriate form of the verb **хостан/хох** 'to want.' For example, for the present the present-future tense of **хостан** is used:

	Singular	Plural
1st	ман...хӯрдан мехоҳам 'I want to eat'	мо...хӯрдан мехоҳем 'we want to eat'
2nd	ту...хӯрдан мехоҳӣ 'you (sg.) want to eat'	шумо...хӯрдан мехоҳед 'you (pl.) want to eat'
3rd	вай...хӯрдан мехоҳад 'he wants to eat'	онҳо...хӯрдан мехоҳанд, 'they want to eat'

Ман дар хона мондан мехоҳам, 'I want to stay at home.'

Again, both the subjunctive auxiliary and the main verb may be negated.

Ман хӯрдан намехоҳам, 'I do not want to eat'
Ман нахӯрдан мехоҳам, 'I want to refrain from eating'
Ман нахӯрдан намехоҳам, 'I don't want to refrain from eating.'

To indicate other tenses, the auxiliary **хостан** is conjugated in the appropriate tense. Like **тавонистан**, **хостан** is a stative verb and cannot be conjugated in the continuous tenses.

Ман ба Муғулистон рафтан хостам, 'I wanted to go to Mongolia.'
Ман хӯрдан нахостам, 'I didn't want to eat.'
Ман нахӯрдан хостам, 'I wanted to refrain from eating.'
Ман нахӯрдан нахостам, 'I didn't want to refrain from eating.'

Note that this construction can only be used when the subject of the main verb is the same as the person desiring the action, that is, when you would say, for example, *I want to go*. To say *I want him to go*, where the subject of the main verb is different from the subject of **хостан**, you must use an object clause (see Chapter 5, Section 2).

In the subjunctive construction the verb **хостан** comes directly after the subject and the present subjunctive of the main verb comes at the end of the sentence. There is no difference in meaning between the non-finite and subjunctive constructions, but the subjunctive construction is preferred if the main verb phrase is very long.

Thus, if the main verb is **хӯрдан** 'to eat, to drink,' the conjugation is:

	Singular	Plural
1st	мехоҳам...хӯрам 'I want to eat'	мехоҳем...хӯрем 'we want to eat'
2nd	мехоҳӣ...хӯрӣ 'you (*sg.*) want to eat'	мехоҳед...хӯред 'you (*pl.*) want to eat'
3rd	мехоҳад...хӯрад 'he wants to eat'	мехоҳанд...хӯранд 'they want to eat'

As with the other forms, both the subjunctive auxiliary and the main verb may be negated.

Ман намехоҳам хӯрам, 'I do not want to eat.'
Ман мехоҳам нахӯрам, 'I want to refrain from eating.'
Ман намехоҳам нахӯрам, 'I don't want to refrain from eating.'

Naturally, just as with the non-finite construction other tenses are formed by conjugating **хостан**:

Ман хостам ба Муғулистон равам, 'I wanted to go to Mongolia.'
Ман нахостам хӯрам, 'I didn't want to eat.'
Ман хостам нахӯрам, 'I wanted to refrain from eating.'
Ман нахостам нахӯрам, 'I didn't want to refrain from eating.'

The other two Tajiki modals are **бояд** 'must' and **шояд** 'should.' They are frozen forms of verbs that have otherwise fallen out of use in all modern Persian dialects; they thus act like adverbs but can take **на-**. The main verb, which can occur in three tenses to indicate various senses of obligation or possibility, comes at the end of the sentence, and between the modal and the main verb come any objects and prepositional phrases that complete the meaning of the verb (such as phrases in **аз** or **ба** with verbs of motion), as well as adverbs closely modifying the main verb (especially ones reinforcing aspect, such as **аллакай** 'already.')

c. Expression of necessity. To indicate a variety of kinds of obligation or necessity arising from inner conviction, Tajiki uses the auxiliary **бояд** 'must.'

1) To indicate that the subject is obligated to perform an action in the future (*I must go, I have to leave, I ought to/should stay*), **бояд** is followed by the present subjunctive of the main verb; it precedes the noun of compound verbs. This construction means 'must, ought.'

	Singular	*Plural*
1st	**ман бояд кунам** 'I must do'	**мо бояд кунем** 'we must do'
2nd	**ту бояд кунӣ** 'you (sg.) must do'	**шумо бояд кунед** 'you (pl.) must do'
3rd	**ӯ бояд кунад** 'he must do'	**онҳо бояд кунанд** 'they must do'

Ман бояд ба хона равам, 'I must go home.'
Шумо чиро бояд кунед? 'What do you have to do?'

The simple negative is formed by adding **на-** to the verb, giving the sense that something shouldn't be done. For the more emphatic sense of prohibition (*must not*), **на-** is prefixed to **бояд**.

Ту бояд дер накунӣ, 'You shouldn't be late.'
Ту набояд дер кунӣ, 'You mustn't be late.'

2) To indicate that the subject was obligated to perform an action in the past (*I had to leave, I ought to/should have stayed*), **бояд** is followed by the past imperfect of the main verb. This construction is best translated as 'had to, should have.' The negative is formed by adding **на-** to the verb (*not to have had to*) or to **бояд** (*should not have*).

	Singular	Plural
1st	ман бояд мекардам 'I had to do'	мо бояд мекардем 'we had to do'
2nd	ту бояд мекардӣ 'you (sg.) had to do'	шумо бояд мекардед 'you (pl.) had to do'
3rd	ӯ бояд мекард 'he had to do'	онҳо бояд мекарданд 'they had to do'

Онҳо бояд ба Душанбе мерафтанд,
'They had to go to Dushanbe.'
Ту дар он ҷо бояд намемондӣ,
'You didn't have to stay there.'
Ту дар он ҷо набояд мемондӣ,
'You shouldn't have stayed there.'

3) To indicate a conjecture that the subject must have performed an action in the past (*He must have left already*), **бояд** is followed by the perfect subjunctive of the main verb. This construction means 'must have' in the sense of being required by the force of circumstances but not known for certain to have occurred, or a conjecture based on evidence and what is reasonable to expect.

	Singular	Plural
1st	ман бояд карда бошам 'I must have done'	мо бояд карда бошем 'we must have done'
2nd	ту бояд карда бошӣ 'you (sg.) must have done'	шумо бояд карда бошед 'you (pl.) must have done'
3rd	ӯ бояд карда бошад 'he must have done'	онҳо бояд карда бошанд 'they must have done'

Вақте ки ман ба хона расидам, вай бояд хобида бошад,
'She must have been sleeping when I got home.'

d. Expression of possibility. To indicate a variety of kinds of possibility, Tajiki uses the auxiliary **шояд** 'might.'

1) To indicate that the subject might perform an action in the future (*I might go*), **шояд** is followed by the present subjunctive of the main verb.

	Singular	Plural
1st	ман шояд кунам 'I might do'	мо шояд кунем 'we might do'
2nd	ту шояд кунӣ 'you (*sg.*) might do'	шумо шояд кунед 'you (*pl.*) might do'
3rd	ӯ шояд кунад 'he might do'	онҳо шояд кунанд 'they might do'

Соли оянда мо шояд ба Париж равем,
'We might go to Paris next year.'

2) To indicate that the subject had the possibility of performing an action in the past (*perhaps I would have gone*), **шояд** is followed by the past imperfect of the main verb. This construction is used to indicate a counterfactual statement or a statement of past possibility and is best translated 'might have, perhaps...would have.'

	Singular	Plural
1st	ман шояд мекардам 'I might have done'	мо шояд мекардем 'we might have done'
2nd	ту шояд мекардӣ 'you (*sg.*) might have done'	шумо шояд мекардед 'you (*pl.*) might have done'
3rd	ӯ шояд мекард 'he might have done'	онҳо шояд мекарданд 'they might have done'

Ту шояд ба ҷояш лағмон мехӯрдӣ,
'You might have eaten *laghman* instead.'
Шояд ман ба Душанбе намерафтам,
'Perhaps I wouldn't have gone to Dushanbe.'

3) To indicate a conjecture that the subject might have performed an action in the past (*He might have left already*), **шояд** is followed by the perfect subjunctive of the main verb. This construction means 'might have' in the sense of a possibility allowed by the force of circumstances, or a conjecture that is weaker than that indicated by **бояд карда бош-** 'must have done.'

	Singular	Plural
1st	ман шояд карда бошам 'I might have done'	мо шояд карда бошем 'we might have done'
2nd	ту шояд карда бошӣ 'you (*sg.*) might have done'	шумо шояд карда бошед 'you (*pl.*) might have done'
3rd	ӯ шояд карда бошад 'he might have done'	онҳо шояд карда бошанд 'they might have done'

Вай шояд аллакай рафта бошад,
'He might have left already.'

7. Verbs requiring care for English learners

a. More on 'to be.' Equational and existential sentences in the present tense were discussed previously in the chapter on nominals (see Chapter 2, Section 7); in other tenses the verb **будан** 'to be' serves for both the predicate endings and **ҳаст** 'there is.' Moreover, a present-tense form of **будан** is used in certain circumstances; it is formed regularly with the present stem **бош** (taken over from the subjunctive):

	Singular	Plural
1st	**мебошам** 'I am'	**мебошем** 'we are'
2nd	**мебошӣ** 'you (*sg.*) are'	**мебошед** 'you (*pl.*) are'
3rd	**мебошад** 'he/she/it is'	**мебошанд** 'they are'

These forms are usually used to add variety to the sentence when there are several clauses in a row that would all use the predicate endings. They are also used following personal possessive markers.

Ман бистуҳафтсолаам, акоям сиюсесола мебошад ва хоҳарам бистсола аст, 'I'm 27 and my big brother is 33, and my little sister is 20.'
Он мошини падарам мебошад, 'That's my father's car.'
Note: Он мошини падари ман аст *is also used to avoid the sequence of personal possessive marker and predicate ending, which is jarring to Tajiki speakers.*

In addition, when a relative clause would cause two or more predicate markers to pile up at the end of the sentence, one of them is replaced by **бош** to prevent awkwardness, since the predicate endings sound unnatural unless they follow nominals. Such sentences can be handled stylistically so as to avoid such a pile-up, but even then **бош** is preferred to prevent repetition. Compare:

Падари Сӯҳроб он марде, ки аз Помир аст, аст.
'Suhrob's father is the man from Pomir.' (*most awkward*)
Падари Сӯҳроб он марде, ки аз Помир мебошад, аст.
'Suhrob's father is the man from Pomir.' (*very awkward*)
Падари Сӯҳроб он марде аст, ки аз Помир аст.
(*too repetitive*)
Падари Сӯҳроб он марде аст, ки аз Помир мебошад.
(*preferred*)

Otherwise **бош** is mostly used in formal written Tajiki.
In addition, the verb **шудан/шав** 'to become' is closely associated with **будан** 'to be.' Its basic meaning is the same as English 'to become,' indicating the change from one condition to another. It is used more widely than 'to become,' often in the same circumstances that spoken English uses 'to get':

Ман бемор будам, 'I was sick.'
Ман бемор шудам, 'I got sick.'

Frequently it is used in the present-future tense more or less as a substitute for **будан**, and as a result it is also so used in the simple past tense. However, **шудан** has the added meaning of an involuntary or passive change, which is in fact the source of its use in forming the passive.
In addition, **шудан** is used to indicate that something is suitable, socially acceptable, or possible. Note that since in many cases such state-

ments are general, the present-future tense forms **мешавад** 'it will do' and **намешавад** 'it won't do' are used (note the use of the past participle of a verb with **шудан** in the last sentence without a passive meaning):

Ана, инаш мешавад, 'Ok, this will do!.'
Ин хел намешавад, '(Acting) this way won't do.'
Аз ин ҷо ба он ҷо рафта намешавад,
'You can't get there from here.'

Finally, to indicate location the expression **ҷойгир аст** 'is located' is used with **дар** 'at': **Бонки Миллӣ дар маркази шаҳр ҷойгир аст**, 'The National Bank is located at the city center.'

b. Доштан 'to have, hold' and гирифтан 'to take, get, obtain.' The verb **доштан** has the basic meaning of 'to take, to hold,' but is mostly used in the sense 'to have' or 'to own.' In this sense it is a stative verb and does not take the prefix **ме-**.

	Singular	Plural
1st	**дорам** 'I have'	**дорем** 'we have'
2nd	**дорӣ** 'you (*sg.*) have'	**доред** 'you (*pl.*) have'
3rd	**дорад** 'he/she/it has'	**доранд** 'they have'

Ман китоб доштам, 'I had a book (books).'
Шумо ин китобро доред? 'Do you have the book?'

However, when **доштан** is used in the concrete sense of holding, taking, or grasping, or when it is part of a compound verb (for example, **дӯст доштан** 'to like'), its present is conjugated in the regular way:

Вай қаламашро медорад, 'She is holding her pencil.'
Ман ин китобро дӯст медорам, 'I like this book.'

Доштан is used to indicate actual possession; existence is indicated by **ҳаст** (**будан** in the past tense). Thus, 'to have' in English does not always correspond to **доштан**.

Дар Тоҷикистон бисёр кӯҳ ҳаст,
'Tajikistan has lots of mountains,
there are many mountains in Tajikistan.'

The verb **гирифтан** is used quite similarly to the English verb *get*. Its basic meaning is 'to take,' but it is also used more broadly in the sense of obtaining or receiving something.

3. Verbs of sensing. Verbs of sensing indicate that a person (or other animal) is sensing something; as in English, there is a difference for seeing and hearing between passive sensing, in which something is simply sensed (*to see, to hear*), and active sensing, in which the subject is paying attention or actively observing something (*to look, to listen*). The Tajiki verbs of sensing are the following:

Sense	Passive	Active
sight	дидан/бин 'to see'	нигоҳ кардан 'to look'
hearing	шунидан/шунав 'to hear'	гӯш кардан 'to listen'
feel	ҳис кардан 'to feel'	ҳис кардан 'to feel'
taste	чашидан/чаш 'to taste'	чашидан 'to taste'
smell	бӯй кардан 'to smell'	бӯй кардан 'to smell'

The passive verbs of sensing all treat the thing being sensed as a direct object. The active verbs, however, make a distinction between actually observing something and expecting to observe something, much as in English. In *I am looking at John*, John is actually in sight, while in *I am looking for John*, I am expecting to see him but he is not in sight. In Tajiki, the former meaning is indicated with **ба**, the latter with the direct object.

Ман Далерро нигоҳ карда истодаам,
'I'm looking/waiting for Daler.'
Ман ба Далер нигоҳ карда истодаам, 'I'm looking at Daler.'
Вай радиоро гӯш карда истодааст, 'He's listening to the radio.'
Вай ба гапам гӯш карда истодааст,
'He's listening to me (literally, my speech).'

In addition to **нигоҳ кардан**, Tajiki has the verb **тамошо кардан** 'to watch.' Unlike English, this verb only takes a direct object.

The English verbs of sensing (except for hearing, for which English uses 'to sound') can also be used to indicate the impression something makes on your senses, such as *You look good, It tastes great,* and *The milk smells sour.* Tajiki verbs of sensing are not used this way. For seeing and hearing the verb **намудан/намо** 'to appear, seem' is used, while for the other senses you say, for example, **Бӯяш бад аст** 'It smells bad' (literally, 'its smell is bad').

Далер шод менамояд, 'Daler seems happy.'
Вай хаста наменамуд, 'She didn't seem tired.'

Similarly, in English the verbs of sensing can be used in an abstract sense to indicate your evaluation of a situation, such as *It looks like John left, Sounds like you've got a problem,* or *It just doesn't feel right.* For these senses you can use the 3rd person singular of **намудан** 'to seem' with an object clause (see Chapter 5 Section 2).

The verbs of sensing are used as in English with **тавонистан** 'to be able' to indicate both *failure* to sense something and *incapacity* to sense something; thus, **Ман онро дида наметавонам** 'I can't see it' can mean either that there is something in the way or the object is not in view, or that the speaker is blind or has weak sight. It is common to express the former meaning with phrases like **Он ба чашмонам/гӯшам нарасид** 'It didn't reach my eyes/ears.'

d. Verbs of posture. The use of the Tajiki verbs **нишастан/шин** 'to sit down,' **хестан/хез** 'to rise, stand up, get up,' and **дароз кашидан/дароз каш** 'to lie down' can be tricky for English speakers. In most tenses Tajiki uses these verbs as you would expect from English.

Зулфия дар лаби дарё нишаст,
'Zulfia sat down at the edge of the river.'
Далер аз курсӣ хест, 'Daler got up from the chair.'
Бобоям дар диван дароз мекашид,
'Grandpa would lie down on the sofa.'

However, in English the present and past progressives of these verbs have two distinct meanings. They can be used to indicate that the process of sitting down, lying down, or standing up is now or was at a given time still ongoing; thus, *Mary's just now sitting down* means that she is in the middle of sitting down (or, idiomatically, that she is in the process of settling in her chair and getting comfortable). For this sense Tajiki uses the present and past continuous tenses. However, the English progressive forms of these verbs much more commonly mean that the action has finished and the person is in the resulting state. Thus, *Mary's sitting at the table right now* means that Mary is seated at the table. For this sense Tajiki uses the present perfect tense (for present time) or the past distant tense (for past time); that is, one says the equivalent of *She has sat down* or *He had lain down.*

Парвиз дар боғ нишастааст, 'Parviz is sitting in the garden.'
Гурбаам дар бом нишаста буд, 'My cat was sitting on the roof.'
Мӯйсафед дар сояи дарахти тут дароз кашидааст,
'The old man is lying in the shade of the mulberry tree.'
Модарам аз сардард дароз кашида буданд,
'Mother was lying down because of a headache.'

In addition, English speakers need to take care in translating the verb 'to stand.' To indicate standing as opposed to walking or running, Tajiki uses the verb **истодан/ист** 'to stand, stay, stop.' On the other hand, to indicate the state of being on one's feet as opposed to sitting or lying down, the verb **рост истодан** 'to be standing, to stand straight' is used. Finally, to indicate that someone is standing after having stood up from a sitting or lying position, the present perfect tense (the past distant tense for times in the past) of **хестан** 'to get up' is used.

Similar considerations hold for other important verbs like **пӯшидан/пӯш** 'to put on, wear'; the meaning of 'wear' is indicated by the present perfect or distant past. Similarly, with **гум шудан** 'to get/ become lost,' one says **гум шудааст** 'he's lost,' rather than **гум мешавад,** which would mean 'he's getting lost, he gets/will get lost.' However, there are many verbs for which the distinction between a change of state and the resulting state is not indicated by aspect. Thus, **хобидан** can mean 'to sleep' and 'to go to sleep,' and both the present perfect **хобидааст** and the present-future **мехобад** mean 'he's sleeping,' while **хобидааст** also means 'he's gone to sleep.' (One also uses such phrases as **Хобаш бурд** 'he went to sleep,' literally 'sleep carried him off.') Other verbs do not use the present perfect for present meanings: Thus, one only says **медонам** 'I know,' not ****донистаам**.

e. Transitive-intransitive pairs of verbs. As discussed in Section 2 above, many verbs in English can be either transitive or intransitive depending on context. This is not true of Tajiki verbs, which are much more often either transitive or intransitive but not both. However, quite often an English verb that has both intransitive and transitive meanings will correspond in Tajiki to two closely related verbs. The most common patterns are as follows:

1) An intransitive verb and its causative form:
гузаштан/гузар 'to pass (*intransitive*)' and **гузарондан** 'to pass (*transitive*), spend (*time*)'

2) A transitive verb and its passive form:
овехтан/овез 'to hang (*transitive*)' and **овехта шудан** 'to be hung, to hang (*intransitive*)'

3) A compound verb with active and passive auxiliaries:
ях кардан/бастан 'to freeze (*transitive*)' and **ях шудан** 'to freeze (*intransitive*)'

However, this is only true of verbs that differ *only* in transitivity. Many transitive English verbs can be used intransitively or in the passive to indicate that the action actually applies reflexively to the subject (or with other idiomatic meanings); this change in meaning is indicated in Tajiki in a wide variety of ways that must be learned individually for each verb. For example, in English 'to prepare' is transitive with a corresponding passive 'to be prepared'; when used intransitively, 'to prepare' actually means 'to prepare oneself.' This last meaning is indicated quite differently in Tajiki:

тайёр кардан 'to prepare (*something;* **ба** for)'
тайёр шудан 'to be prepared (**ба** for)'
тайёри дидан 'to prepare (*oneself;* **ба** for)'
(lit., to see/undergo preparation)

Ман барои дарс иншое тайёр кардам,
   'I prepared an essay for class.'
Хӯроки Наврӯзӣ тайёр шудааст,
   'The food was prepared for **Navruz**.'
Ман ба имтиҳон тайёрӣ дидам,
   'I prepared for the test.'

Chapter 4 Adverbs and Particles

1. Adverbs and adverbial phrases

Adverbs are words that modify verbs (*ran quickly*), adjectives (*very green*), and other adverbs (*very quickly*). Adverbs that modify adjectives and other adverbs are placed immediately before the word they modify, and they should present no problems for English learners. Comparatives and superlatives of adverbs are formed in the same way as for adjectives. Adverbs and adverbial phrases that modify verbs fall into four main groups as in English, adverbials of time, place, manner, and quantity.

a. Adverbials of time. Tajiki has numerous simple adverbs of time. The most important ones to indicate past time (and thus occurring with past-tense verb forms) are:

дирӯз 'yesterday' (with the colloquial form дина),
дишаб 'last night'
парерӯз 'the day before yesterday'
парешаб 'two nights ago'
порсол/порина 'last year'
парерсол 'the year before last'
навакак/ҳозиракак 'just now, recently'

Of course, the adverbs имрӯз 'today' and имшаб 'tonight' can be used with the past tense if referring to times earlier today or tonight. For present and future time, the following adverbs are quite common:

алҳол/ҳоло/ҳозир 'now'   зуд 'soon'
дарҳол 'immediately'   имрӯз 'today'
имшаб 'tonight'   фардо 'tomorrow'
имсол 'this year'   пасфардо 'day after tomorrow'

Many adverbs of time refer simply to parts of a day or year and frequently have a habitual sense. Examples include:

рӯзона 'in the daytime, daily'
шабона 'in the nighttime, nightly'
бегоҳӣ 'in the evening'
пагоҳӣ 'in the morning'
нисфирӯзӣ 'noontime'
пешинӣ 'at noon'

Note that these adverbs can also be used as adjectives. Other important adverbs of time include: **ҳамеша** 'always,' **зуд-зуд/тез-тез** 'often,' **гоҳ-гоҳ** 'sometimes,' **баъзан** 'now and then, on occasion, sometimes,' and **ҳаргиз/ҳеҷ гоҳ** with a negative verb, 'never.' Also important are the following:

ҳанӯз 'not yet' (*used with a negative verb*)
боз 'still'   **муваққатан** 'for the time being'
аллакай 'already,'   **фавран** 'immediately'
тамоман 'finally'   **ба наздикӣ** 'soon, recently'

In addition, there are several ways of forming adverbial phrases indicating time:

1) With units of time, 'last' is **гузашта** 'past,' 'this' is **ин**, and 'next' is **оянда** 'coming': **соли гузашта** 'last year.'

2) To indicate a given amount of time in the past or preceding the time of reference, the amount of time is followed by the adverb **пеш** 'front, ago': **ду рӯз пеш** 'two days ago/before.'

3) To indicate a given amount of time later than a given time (whether in the past or the future), the amount of time follows the preposition **баъд** or **пас** 'after, later' with izofat: **баъди як ҳафта** 'after one week, a week later.', **пас аз як сол** 'after a year, a year later.' The last word often takes the possessive suffix **-аш** when the phrase indicates a period after a previously-mentioned time: **баъди як ҳафтааш** 'a week after that.'

To indicate a specific day of the week, the name of the day must be preceded by **рӯз**, which takes izofat: **рӯзи душанбе** '(on) Monday.' (This is necessary because many places are named after the day of the week on which the local market day falls, such as **Душанбе** and **Панҷшанбе**, the major bazaar in Khujand; without **рӯз** the name of the day might be mistaken for the name of a place.) Similarly, the month or year in which something happened must follow **моҳ** 'month' or **сол** 'year' with izofat. With all of these expressions, the preposition **дар** 'in, on' is optional: **рӯзи душанбе/дар рӯзи душанбе** '(on) Monday,' **моҳи июл/дар моҳи июл** 'in July,' **соли ду ҳазор/дар соли ду ҳазор** 'in 2000.'

> **Шумо (дар) моҳи июл дар Маскав будед? /**
> **(Дар) моҳи июл Шумо дар Маскав будед?**
> 'Were you in Moscow in July?'

> **Шумо (дар) соли дуҳазорум дар Маскав набудед? /**
> **(Дар) соли дуҳазорум Шумо дар Маскав набудед?**
> 'Weren't you in Moscow in 2000?'

Most adverbs of time and time phrases are placed either at the very beginning of the sentence or immediately following the subject:

> **Ман дирӯз хеле хаста будам / Дирӯз ман хеле хаста будам**,
> 'Yesterday I was very tired.'

> **Мо соли гузашта дар Муғулистон будем /**
> **Соли гузашта мо дар Муғулистон будем**,
> 'Last year we were in Mongolia.'

> **Вай ду рӯз пеш бемор буд / Ду рӯз пеш вай бемор буд**,
> 'He was sick two days ago.'

> **Мо баъди як ҳафтааш дар Душанбе будем /**
> **Баъди як ҳафтааш мо дар Душанбе будем**,
> 'A week later (after that) we were in Dushanbe.'

However, time markers used to indicate on which day or in which month an event falls come right before the verb:

> **Зодрӯзи ӯ дар моҳи июл буд**, 'Her birthday was in July.'
> **Зодрӯзи ӯ дирӯз буд**, 'Her birthday was yesterday.'

The names of the days of the week (which are not capitalized in Tajiki) are:

якшанбе	Sunday	панҷшанбе	Thursday
душанбе	Monday	ҷумъа	Friday
сешанбе	Tuesday	шанбе	Saturday
чоршанбе	Wednesday		

There are several systems of months in Tajiki. While the Islamic solar calendar, Islamic lunar calendar, and traditional Persian calendar might be encountered in various circumstances, the most commonly-used calendar is the Western calendar, borrowed from Russian. (The Tajiki and English names of the months are similar but not identical because the Tajiki month names come ultimately from Greek, the English ultimately from Latin.) Because the month names are borrowed from Russian, they are stressed as in Russian; the stress is indicated below with underlining. (Thus, only **август** differs from normal Tajiki stress on nouns.) Note that the names of the months are not capitalized in Tajiki.

ян<u>вар</u>	January	и<u>юл</u>	July
фев<u>рал</u>	February	<u>ав</u>густ	August
ма<u>рт</u>	March	сент<u>я</u>бр	September
ап<u>рел</u>	April	окт<u>я</u>бр	October
м<u>ай</u>	May	но<u>я</u>бр	November
и<u>юн</u>	June	дек<u>а</u>бр	December

b. Adverbials of place and direction. Tajiki adverbials of place are prepositional phrases for locations; there are no simple adverbs of place like English *home*. They are placed after the subject.

The nouns used in compound prepositions, however, can be used by themselves or with the preposition **6a** to make adverbials of direction. For example:

Вай поён рафт, 'He went down.'
Ман ба поён афтодам, 'I fell down.'
Вай боло давид, 'She ran up.'
Он сӯ паред! 'Jump over!'
Ин сӯ нигоҳ кун! 'Look this way!'
Пеш равед! 'Move along!'

c. Adverbials of manner. In many cases Tajiki adverbs of manner are simply adjectives used adverbially, like in the English *He ran hard*, though this is much more common in Tajiki than in English. While Tajiki does have some adverbial suffixes, there is no equivalent to English suffixes like *-ly*, *-wise*, or *-way* that must be used for almost all adverbs. Adverbials of manner tend to come immediately before the verb.

Certain adverbial suffixes are used with Arabic loanwords, however, particularly *-ан*:

ақалан 'at least' **умуман** 'in general, overall'
аксаран 'mostly, generally' **маъмулан** 'usually'
такроран 'repeatedly' **одатан** 'usually, customarily'
феълан 'currently' **комилан** 'completely'

d. Adverbials of quantity. The most important adverbs of quantity are:

ин қадар 'this much,' **он қадар** 'that much,'
як қадар 'some,' **андак** 'a little,'
бисёр 'much,' **беш** 'more,'
каме 'a little,' **камакак** 'very little'
чӣ қадар 'how much/little!'

When a sentence contains all four types of adverbials, the adverbials of time and manner occur in the sentence as described above, while adverbials of place tend to come between the subject or the adverbial of time (if it follows the subject) and adverbs of manner, either before or after direct and indirect objects.

e. Indefinites. Indefinite pronouns are words like *anybody*, *everyone*, *something*, and *nowhere* that are used to refer to unspecified people, places, or things; indefinite adverbs are such words as *anyhow* and *some time*. Tajiki also has indefinite adjectives meaning *some kind of*, etc. In English there are five series of indefinite pronouns and adverbs; four of them are formed by prefixing *any*, *some*, *no*, and *every* to words like *body*, *one*, *thing*, *where*, *time*, and *how* that indicate the category of the indefinite word, while the fifth is formed by suffixing the corresponding interrogatives with *ever* (*whoever*, *whenever*, etc.). Their Tajiki equivalents are simpler, but because they do not match up exactly with any of the English series they require some explanation.

There are three series of Tajiki indefinite pronouns and adverbs, all formed from the base nouns **кас** 'person,' **чиз** 'thing,' **ҷо** 'place,' **вақт** 'time,' **тавр** 'manner,' **бор** 'time, occasion,' **гуна** 'type,' and **қадар** 'amount.'

	Unspecified	Negative	Universal
Person	касе	ҳеҷ кас(е)	ҳар кас
Thing	чизе	ҳеҷ чиз(е)	ҳар чиз
Place	ҷое	ҳеҷ ҷо(е)	ҳама ҷо/ҳар ҷо
Time	вақте	ҳеҷ вақт	ҳар вақт
Manner	тавре/хел	ҳеҷ тавр/ҳеҷ хел	ҳар тавр/ҳар хел
Occasion	боре	ягон бор	ҳар бор
Type	гуна (rare)	ҳеҷ гуна	ҳар гуна
Amount	қадар	ҳеҷ қадар	ҳар қадар

1) Indefinite nouns and adverbs proper (here called *unspecified*) are formed with the clitic **-е** showing indefiniteness, which can be emphasized or replaced with **як** 'one' or **ягон** 'several, some' before the base noun. (When used as direct objects, they must take **-ро**.) These words correspond to the English *some-* and *any*-series in most of their uses, but can also be used in certain circumstances where English uses a word from the *no*-series.

The words of the *some*-series are almost always expressed in Tajiki in this way:

> **Ман чизеро шунидам,** 'I heard something.'
> **Ягон вақт мекунам,** 'I will do it some time.'
> **Чизеро мебинӣ?** 'Do you see something?'
> (*Also can mean, 'Do you see anything?'*)
> **Агар Шумо касеро бинед, ба ман гӯед,**
> 'If you see someone (anyone), tell me.'

However, in a question like "Do you see something?" above, a negative indefinite can be used for emphasis.

> **Ҳеҷ чизеро мебинӣ?**
> 'Do you see anything at all?, Don't you see anything?'

The *any*-series is harder to translate because it has several distinct uses in English. The *some*-series is used for indefinite but specific (known to some extent by the speaker but not the listener); the basic use of the *any*-series is roughly to indicate indefinite and non-specific (unknown or unspecified by either speaker or listener), in which case it is translated with an unspecified indefinite just like the *some*-series.

Чизеро мебинӣ? 'Do you see <u>something/anything</u>?'
Агар Шумо <u>касеро</u> бинед, ба ман гӯед,
'If you see <u>someone/anyone</u>, tell me.'

However, the *any*-series is also used in negative sentences in English, in which case Tajiki can use either an unspecified or a negative indefinite.

Ман <u>касеро/ҳеҷ кас(е)ро</u> надидам,
'I didn't see anybody/I saw nobody.' (*Direct negative*)
Вай фикр накард, ки онҳо <u>чизеро</u> дидаанд,
'He didn't think that they saw anything.' (*Indirect negative*)
Вай фикр кард, ки онҳо <u>ҳеҷ чизеро</u> надидаанд,
'He thought that they didn't see anything.' (*Indirect negative*)

Finally, the *any*-series is used in comparisons (*better than anyone*) and to indicate a free choice (*anywhere you might go*); the first of these is indicated by **аз ҳама** 'than all, of all' and the comparative form of the adjective, while the second requires a universal indefinite in Tajiki. (A useful test is to replace the *any*-word with a corresponding *every*-word; if the sentence makes sense with very little change in meaning, then you should use the universal indefinite in Tajiki.)

Далер аз ҳама ҷасуртар аст, 'Daler is braver than anyone.'
Ҳар касе метавонад китоб нависад, 'Anyone can write a book.'

2) Negative indefinites almost always correspond to the English *no*-series. They are formed by putting **ҳеҷ** before the base noun and optionally adding **-е**; the verb must be negative except when the negative indefinite is being used emphatically in a question, as discussed in 1a.

Касе/ҳеҷ кас(е) наомад, 'Nobody came.'

Ман ба ҷое/ҳеҷ ҷо(е) нарафтам, 'I didn't go anywhere.'

3) Universal indefinites usually correspond to the *every*-series; their use with *any*-words was discussed in 1b. They are formed by putting **ҳар** 'each' or **ҳама** 'all, every' before the base noun; for emphasis you can use **ҳар як**, which has somewhat the sense of 'each and every' or 'every single.' When a universal indefinite is used as a subject, the verb must be singular.

Ман ҳар як китобатонро хондам,
'I read every single one of your books.'
Вай ҳар як чизро бӯй карда харид,
'He smelled each and everything before he bought it.'
Дар ҳама ҷо борон борида истодааст,
'It's raining everywhere.'

The best rule for translating English sentences with words in the *ever*-series (*whoever, wherever,* etc.) is to replace it with the word from the other series that best conveys the same meaning and translate it as that word following the discussion above.

Sentences can contain more than one indefinite pronoun or adverb. If the sentence is negative, an *unspecified* indefinite cannot precede a *negative* indefinite. Thus, the following sentences are fine:

Касе чизеро надид/
Ҳеҷ кас чизеро надид/
Ҳеҷ кас ҳеҷ чизро надид
all meaning 'No one saw anything,'
  but not:
* **Касе ҳеҷ чизро надид.**

Indefinite pronouns used with *else*, such as *something else*, can have two distinct meanings, *something additional* ('I'm still hungry—give me something else') or *something different* ('I'm not in the mood for chicken—let's have something else'). These are translated differently in Tajiki: *Something additional* is **боз як чизи дигар**, while *something different* is **як чизи дигар**.

2. Introductory phrases

Introductory phrases are words and phrases used to connect or show the relationship of a sentence to the preceding sentences. There is a wide range of very common introductory set phrases in prose whose proper use is important for advanced learners (such as English "Be that as it may...," "As quickly became apparent...," or "However much one might wish otherwise..."). For beginning learners, however, it is only necessary to know the most basic ones:

бо вуҷуди ин/он 'however, nonetheless'
инчунин, ҳамчунин 'also'
новобаста ба ин/он 'besides (*indicating contrast*)'
дар баробари ин/он 'besides (*indicating similarity*)'
аз як тараф/сӯ...аз тарафи/сӯйи дигар
'on the one hand...on the other'
илова ба ин, ба замми ин (*formal*) 'moreover, in addition'
дар ин сурат 'in this case'
дар он сурат 'in that case'
ба ибораи дигар 'that is to say'
хушбахтона 'fortunately'
бадбахтона 'unfortunately'
барои ҳамин/ҳамон 'therefore'
масалан 'for example, thus'
бинобар ин 'thus (*because of this*)'
ба дин сон, ин тавр 'thus, hence'
дар натиҷа 'as a result'
ҳамин тавр, ба ҳамин тариқб ҳамин хел
'so, in the same way'
ба ростӣ, дар воқеъ, ҳақиқатан 'indeed'
дар ҳақиқат 'in fact'
хулоса (*more common*), **алқисса** 'in conclusion'
дар охир(ин), ниҳоят 'finally'
дар муқоиса 'in contrast'

3. Interrogative particles

There are several particles used to indicate various types of questions. The particles **магар** and **оё** come at the beginning of a sentence to indicate a yes-no question; **магар** is almost always used with negative sentences, while **оё** can be used with any sentence. They are highly literary.

Оё ман хобидаам? 'Am I sleeping?'
Магар инро намедонистӣ? 'Didn't you know this?'

The particle **-мӣ** is suffixed to the verb to indicate a yes-no question. It is a colloquial form used only in the northern dialects under the influence of Uzbek and is considered extremely substandard by many Tajiks; foreign speakers should avoid it.

Овозро шунидед-мӣ? 'Did you hear the noise?'

The particle **-чӣ** is used to indicate a follow-up question with the sense of "and what about..." or "and how about...?"

- **Шумо аз Душанбеед?** 'Are you from Dushanbe?'
- **Ҳа, шумо-чӣ?** 'Yes, and how about you?'

The particle **-a** is suffixed to the verb to indicate a question meant to confirm a suspicion or to seek assurance. It often corresponds in meaning to the English "tag questions" at the end of sentences like "You're going to work now, *aren't you?*" and "He didn't go to the store, *did he?*"

Шумо нонро хӯрдед-а?
'You ate the bread, didn't you?'
Ман бояд ин корро кунам-а?
'I should do this, right (shouldn't I)?'

4. Interjections

Interjections are words like *yes, no, well, hmm, ugh,* and *oops* that are not grammatically related to the rest of the sentence and usually serve to express emotion. Besides the interjections listed in Chapter 1 Section 7.2f, the following are important in Tajiki: **ҳа/бале/оре** 'yes,' **не/ на** 'no,' **хуб** 'well,' **бубин** 'see here,' and **афсӯс** 'alas.'

Chapter 5 Compound and Complex Sentences

Phrases can be joined into clauses, clauses into sentences, and sentences into larger sentences similarly in English and Tajiki, with conjunctions or by forming a relative clause (relativization). There are two types of conjunctions: *Subordinating conjunctions* make one sentence logically and grammatically dependent on the other, while *coordinating conjunctions* do not; *relative clauses* are used to modify nouns by subordinating to the noun an independent clause about it. Examples of subordinating conjunctions in English are *when* (*When he gets here, we'll eat*), *after* (*We left after John played the piano with a hammer*), *although* (*Although he was rich, he only shopped at second-hand stores*), and *because* (*We love her because she's unintentionally very funny*). Relative clauses are like the following: *the man whom I saw*, *the woman who's painting the house*, and *the house that Jack built*. Coordinating conjunctions form *compound sentences* (sentences composed of more than one independent clause); sentences with relative and subordinate clauses are called *complex sentences*. Various types of compound and complex sentences in Tajiki will be discussed in the order of grammatical complexity.

1. Coordinating conjunctions and compound sentences

English coordinating conjunctions include *and, but, yet, (either)...or* and *nor*: *John went home and I went to the store; April has come but it's still snowing; It's freezing yet he's not wearing a coat; Either John goes or I go; He's not happy, nor is he healthy.* The basic Tajiki coordinating conjunctions are **ва (-у)** 'and,' **ё** 'or,' **аммо/вале/лекин** 'but, however,' **ҳам...ҳам** 'both...and,' **ё...ё** 'either...or,' **на...на** 'neither...nor,' and **на танҳо/на фақат...балки** 'not only...but also.' All of these are used to join clauses in sentences, but only the first two can be used to join words into phrases as well. Note that when used as part of **на...на**, **на** does not immediately precede the verb but instead immediately follows the place of the subject.

Ман китоб хондам ва Парвиз нома навишт,
'I read a book and Parviz wrote a letter.'

Ҳар бегоҳ Парвиз рӯзнома ё китоб мехонд,
'Every evening Parviz would read a newspaper or a book.'
Ман китобатро хондам, аммо онро нафаҳмидам,
'I read your book, but I didn't understand it.'
Ман ҳам китоб хонда, ҳам мусиқӣ гӯш карда истода будам,
'I was both reading a book and listening to music.'
Ё ман ба он ҷо меравам, ё вай ба ин ҷо меояд,
'Either I will go there or she will come here.'
Ман на китобро хондаам, на филмро дидаам,
'I have neither read the book nor seen the movie.'

If a sentence containing **ё…ё**, **на…на**, or **ҳам…ҳам** uses the same verb in both parts, one of the verbs must be omitted; in most cases the second verb is the one omitted:

Ҳар бегоҳ Парвиз ё рӯзнома мехонад, ё китоб,
'Every morning Parviz either reads a newspaper or a book.'
Ё ман беморам, ё ту, 'Either I'm sick or you (are).'
Онҳо на ба хонаашон мераванд, на ба мактаб,
'They will neither go home nor to school.'
Онҳо ҳам забон меомӯзанд, ҳам адабиёт,
'They study both language and literature.'

In addition, to prevent repetitiveness when there is a series of clauses strung together with **ё…ё**, you can use **ё ки** and **ё ин ки** 'or else' before the second or later clauses.

Ё ман ба он ҷо меравам, ё ки вай ба ин ҷо меояд, ё ин ки мо дар Хуҷанд вомехӯрем, 'Either I'll go there, or she'll come here, or else we'll meet in Khojand.'

2. Object clauses

Object clauses (also called complement clauses) are those like *that you like her* in *I know that you like her*, in which the dependent sentence as a whole is the object of a verb. In English object clauses are indicated with *that*, which can be omitted, or *if/whether*: *I don't know if he went, I wonder whether he will come back*. Object clauses are indicated in Tajiki with **ки** (which is always unstressed) after the independent clause; in Tajiki orthography, **ки** is set off from the preceding word with a comma. Use of the subjunctive in the dependent clause indicates possibility, doubt or uncertainty; it is used in many cases where English would use *if/whether*.

> **Ман медонам, ки вай ошиқи Дилбар аст,**
> 'I know he's Dilbar's sweetheart.'
> **Ман намедонам, ки вай ошиқи Дилбар аст,**
> 'I don't know that he's Dilbar's sweetheart.'
> **Ман намедонам, ки вай ошиқи Дилбар бошад,**
> 'I don't know if he's Dilbar's sweetheart.'

If the dependent sentence names an action in the past, the dependent verb must be in the distant past tense if the time is unspecified; the simple past can only be used if the time is specified. (Note that if the sentence implies second-hand knowledge, a reportative verb form must be used instead.)

> **Вай фикр кард, ки ман вайро дида будам,**
> 'He thought I had seen him.'
> *(No time specified, so the distant past must be used.)*
> **Вай фикр кард, ки ҳафтаи гузашта ман вайро дидам,**
> 'He thought that I saw him last week.'
> *(Time specified, so simple past is used.)*
> **Вай гуфт, ки ҳафтаи гузашта маро дар мағоза дидааст,**
> 'He said that he saw me in the store last week.'
> *(The sentence implies knowledge by hearsay and thus requires a reportative form like the present perfect.)*

If the object clause does not have a direct object, it is possible to use an infinitive phrase in place of an object clause; the subject of the object clause is shown by a personal possessive marker on the infinitive, which being definite must take **-ро**.

> **Мо медонем, ки Шумо ба Душанбе рафтед,**
> 'We know you went to Dushanbe.'
> • **Мо ба Душанбе рафтанатонро медонем.**
> **Мо медонем, ки Шумо ба Душанбе меравед,**
> 'We know you're going to Dushanbe.'
> • **Мо ба Душанбе рафтанатонро медонем.**

Note that the simple infinitive shows no information at all about tense, so that the two sentences above with object clauses have the same equivalent when using an infinitive clause. Intention can be shown if necessary with the future participle and **будан**, such as **рафтанӣ будан** 'to intend to go.'

Мо ба Душанбе рафтанӣ буданатонро медонем,
'We know you intend(ed) to go to Dushanbe.'

The verbs **гуфтан** 'to say, tell' and **пурсидан** 'to ask' are ambiguous with object clauses in *colloquial* Tajiki, in which, as in English, they can have the meanings of ordering or requesting an action: *I told him to go, I asked her to leave*. The sense of an order or suggestion is shown with the present subjunctive in an object clause, which as mentioned above can also indicate possibility or doubt. (In formal Tajiki, however, the verbs **хоҳиш кардан** 'to wish, ask for' and **талаб кардан** 'to demand' are used instead.)

Мо ба Парвиз гуфтем, ки вай ба Душанбе равад,
'We told Parviz that he might go to Dushanbe; we told Parviz to go to Dushanbe.'
Мо аз Парвиз пурсидем, ки вай ба Душанбе равад,
'We asked Parviz if he might/would go to Dushanbe; we asked Parviz to go to Dushanbe.'

The exact sense is determined from context. Note that with these verbs, use of an infinitive phrase in place of an object clause is further ambiguous for tense.

Мо аз Парвиз ба Душанбе рафтанашро пурсидем,
'We asked Parviz to go to Dushanbe, we asked Parviz if he had gone/was going/would go to Dushanbe.'

If the object of the main sentence is not the whole subordinate sentence but only one element of it, such as *We know when he left*, the question word must be used in addition to the particle **ки**. Unlike English, interrogatives are used only to ask questions, not to show subordination; the English use with an infinitive is roughly equivalent to a subjunctive in the Tajiki subordinate clause:

Мо аз Парвиз пурсидем, ки ӯ кай ба Душанбе меравад.
'We asked Parviz when he is going to Dushanbe.'
Мо аз Парвиз пурсидем, ки ӯ ба кучо меравад.
'We asked Parviz where he is going.'
Мо аз ӯ пурсидем, ки бастаро ба кучо монем.
'We asked him where to put the package.'

3. Subjunctive auxiliary constructions

As mentioned previously, the subjunctive is used to indicate that an action is not actual but rather potential, projected, expected, desired, necessary, possible, or contingent on another action. An appropriate subjunctive auxiliary is used to express most of these modifications of the main action or state; the combination of the auxiliary and the subjunctive form of the main verb then expresses the speaker's desired modification of the verb. The most important auxiliary constructions with the subjunctive apart from the four modal auxiliaries are as follows.

Uncertainty	**фикр кардан**	'to think (whether)'
Compulsion	**мачбур будан**	'to be compelled to'
Possibility	**мумкин аст**	'it is possible'
Preference	**беҳтар аст**	'it is better'
Necessity	**лозим аст**	'it is necessary'
Intent	**то**	'so that, in order to'
Apprehension	**мабодо**	'beware, I fear'
Permission	**бигзор (то)**	'allow'
Wish	**кошки**	'would that'
Condition	**набошад** 'if so,' **ҳарчанд** 'although'	

a. Uncertainty. One way to express uncertainty is through the compound verb **фикр кардан** 'to think' in the present or past continuous tense; it is followed by an object clause with its verb in the present subjunctive.

Фикр карда истодааст, ки ба Душанбе равад ё наравад.
'He is thinking/ uncertain whether or not to go to Dushanbe.'
Фикр карда истода буд, ки ин хӯрокро хӯрад ё нахӯрад,
'He was uncertain whether to eat.'
Фикр карда истодааст, ки китобаш дар кучо бошад,
'He is uncertain where his book is.'

b. Compulsion or External Obligation. Obligation that does not arise from the speaker's personal convictions, but rather from imposition by another person or compulsion by the force of circumstances, is expressed by conjugating the auxiliary **маҷбур будан** 'to be obliged, compelled, forced to' in the simple present tense; it appears early in the sentence, usually immediately after the subject. The main verb appears at the end of the sentence in the present subjunctive. Other elements of the sentence may fill in the gap between the two verbal elements.

> **Ман маҷбурам ба духтур равам,** 'I must go to the doctor.'
> **Дилбар маҷбур аст мошинашро фурӯшад,**
> 'Dilbar must sell her car.'
> **Онҳо маҷбуранд таслим шаванд,**
> 'They are being forced to surrender.'

The past tense of **будан** or **шудан** is used with **маҷбур** to form the past tense expression of obligation; the subjunctive is unchanged.

> **Ман маҷбур будам ба духтур равам,**
> 'I was compelled to go to the doctor.'
> **Дилбар маҷбур шуд мошинашро фурӯшад,**
> 'Dilbar had to/was forced to sell her car.'
> **Онҳо маҷбур буданд таслим шаванд,**
> 'They were forced to surrender.'

c. Possibility. For the expression of possibility or permission, **мумкин аст** 'it is possible' is used; in colloquial Tajiki **аст** is often omitted. **Мумкин аст** usually precedes the subject.

> **Мумкин бароям?** 'May I go out?'
> **Мумкин равӣ,** 'You may go.'
> **Мумкин аст Зулфия занг занад,** 'Zulfia may call.'

In the colloquial language the main verb comes first in the sentence as an infinitive; the subject is indicated with the appropriate possessive suffix:

> **Баромаданам мумкин?** 'May I go out?'
> **Рафтанат мумкин,** 'You may go.'

d. Preference. Preference is expressed by **беҳтар аст** 'it is better,' which is not conjugated to agree with the subject of the sentence (that is, it is a frozen form). **Беҳтар аст** usually precedes the subject.

Беҳтар аст ман ба хона равам,
'It is better that I go home, I'd better go home.'
Беҳтар аст хобӣ, 'It is better that you sleep, you'd better sleep.'
Беҳтар аст мо кор кунем, 'It is better that we work, we'd better work.'

The negative form is **Беҳтар аст...наравам** 'It is better that I not go.' The double negative **Беҳтар нест...наравам** 'It is not better that I not go' is also acceptable.

In the colloquial language, the 3rd singular possessive suffix **-аш** replaces **аст**.

Беҳтараш наравам, 'I'd better not go.'
Беҳтараш хӯрам, 'I'd better eat.'

In addition, as with **мумкин,** in the colloquial language the main verb comes first in the sentence as an infinitive; the subject is indicated with the appropriate possessive suffix. In this construction **беҳтар** occurs without **аст** or **-аш**:

Нарафтанам беҳтар, 'I'd better not go.'
Хӯрданам беҳтар, 'I'd better eat.'

e. Necessity. To indicate necessity, the impersonal form **лозим аст** 'to be necessary' is used as a frozen form; it usually precedes the subject.

Лозим аст ман равам, 'It is necessary that I go, I have to go.'
Лозим аст шабҳо кор кунад,
'It was necessary that he work nights, he had to work nights.'

As with **мумкин аст,** in the colloquial language the main verb comes first in the sentence as an infinitive; the subject is indicated with the appropriate possessive suffix:

Рафтанам лозим аст, 'I have to go.'
Гуфтанаш лозим аст, 'She has to tell.'
Карданамон лозим аст, 'We have to do it.'

The past tense of **мумкин аст**, **беҳтар аст**, and **лозим аст** is formed by replacing **аст** with **буд** and putting the the main verb in the past imperfect instead of the subjunctive; infinitives are unchanged:

Мумкин буд мерафтам/Рафтанам мумкин буд,
'It was possible that I would go.'
Лозим буд мерафт/Рафтанаш лозим буд,
'It was necessary that she go, she had to go.'

f. Intent. To indicate purpose, **то** 'so that, in order to' is used. Sentences with **то** are complex, consisting of two clauses. The first expresses a present or past action, the second its reason; the second clause begins with **то** and ends with the main verb in the subjunctive.

то равам 'so that I go, in order for me to go'
Вай тирезаро пӯшид, то хобад, 'She closed the window in order to get to sleep *(so that she could/might sleep).*'
Мо ба Миср меравем, то аҳромро бинем,
'We're going to Egypt to see the pyramids.'

To indicate trying to avoid the action, the subordinate verb can be made negative, i.e., **то наравам** 'so that I not go, in order for me not to go.'

Дузд дар сояи бино истод, то ӯро касе набинад,
'The thief stood in the shadow of the building in order not to be seen.'

Sentences with **то** can be transformed into simple sentences as follows:

1. Make the verb of the second clause an infinitive;
2. Replace **то** with **барои**;
3. Put the **барои** phrase after the subject.
   Example:
Ман дучарха харидам, то ба донишгоҳ равам,
'I bought a bicycle to go to school.'
Ман барои ба донишгоҳ рафтан дучарха харидам,
'I bought a bicycle to go to school' *(literally, 'for going to school').*

g. Apprehension. мабодо 'beware, I fear'

The conjunction **мабодо** is placed at the beginning of a clause to give a warning or indicate an undesirable circumstance or action; the verb is in the present subjunctive for present or future time and the perfect subjunctive for past time. **Мабодо** is difficult to translate by itself but carries the flavor of 'beware, I fear, I hope not, take care, be careful.' The clause with **мабодо** can stand on its own as an independent sentence, often with a sense rather like that of "or else..." left hanging, or it can be completed with another clause introduced by **ки**:

> **Мабодо дар хона набошад,**
> 'I hope he's not at home; I fear he's at home.'
> **Мабодо ӯ омада бошад,**
> 'I hope he hasn't arrived yet; I fear he's arrived.'
> **Мабодо ба хона надарой,**
> 'Be careful—don't go in the house...'
> **Мабодо ба хона надарой, ки дар он ҷо саги газанда ҳаст,**
> 'Be careful not to go in the house, there's a dog in there that bites.'

h. Permission. бигзор (то) 'allow, let'

The conjunction **бигзор то** (from **би** indicating the subjunctive or imperative in older Persian and **гузоштан/гузор** 'to put') introduces a clause in the present subjunctive and is used to indicate permission or an oblique command; in colloquial speech то is very often omitted. (In very colloquial speech it is replaced with the imperative **мон(ед)**, from **мондан/мон** 'to put, place.') It is best translated as 'Let...' in two of the three main senses this construction has in English: It indicates explicit permission or release from constraint ("Let him go" in the sense of "Set him free") and dismissal ("Let him be gone" in the sense of "Off with him!"), but not a suggestion or insistence on action ("Let's go," which is translated by the bare present subjunctive). These two senses are distinguished in Tajiki by intonation and pacing: Release is indicated by a pause after **бигзор (то)**, while in a clause of dismissal the entire clause is spoken as a single unit. Thus we have:

> **Бигзор, равад!** 'Let him go!'
> **Бигзор равад!** 'Let him be gone! Off with him!'
> **Равем,** 'Let's go, we should go'

Бигзор то бигирям, чун абр дар баҳорон
К-аз шавқ нола хезад, рӯзи бидоҳи ёрон.
Let me weep like the clouds in springtime,
That from love a wail break forth the day lovers part.

The following subordinating conjunctions do not govern the subjunctive.

i. Wish. кошки 'would that, if only'
The conjunction **кошки** is used to express a strong wish; the verb is in the past imperfect to indicate past time and in the present-future to indicate present or future time. In more literary Tajiki the form **кош** is used instead.

Кошки ман дар Тоҷикистон мебодам,
'Would that I were in Tajikistan, How I wish I was in Tajikisan!'
Кошки ӯ дар ин ҷо мешуд/буд, 'If only he were here!'
Кош ман ӯро медидам, 'Would that I had seen her.'

j. Condition. набошад 'if so,' **ҳарчанд** 'although'
The conjunction **набошад** 'if so' is used to express the consequence of a condition; it is followed by the appropriate form of the verb. (Note that there is no single form in Tajiki corresponding to English *if not*.)

Набошад ман пагоҳ шумо мебинам,
'If so, I will see you tomorrow.'
Набошад шумо худатон кунед, 'If so, do it yourself.'

The conjunction **ҳарчанд** 'although' is followed by a verb in the past imperfect for past time and the present-future otherwise:

Ҳарчанд ӯ медонист, худро ба нодонӣ зад,
'Although he knew, he made himself out to be in the dark.'

In very colloquial Tajiki people often say **ҳарчанд ки**, but this is considered improper since in strict usage **ки** must join two clauses.

4. Relative clauses

Relative clauses modify nouns in a larger sentence; thus, in *The man who hit me ran away*, "who hit me" is a relative clause modifying "the man." In English, relative clauses are indicated with the relative pronouns *who(m), that*, and *which* (*The woman who saw me, the woman whom I saw, the car that I bought*, and *the house, which burned down*). In Tajiki there is one relativizer (word indicating a relative clause), the conjunction **ки**, which is never stressed; thus, unlike English Tajiki does not have special relative pronouns. Note that in English the relative pronoun can be omitted if it refers to the direct object of the relative clause: In *the man whom I saw, whom* can be omitted because it fills the place of the direct object of the verb *saw*, thus: *the man I saw*. (Note that you cannot omit *who* in *the man who saw me*; it indicates the subject of *saw*.) In Tajiki, however, you must always use **ки**; it can never be omitted.

English distinguishes between *restrictive* and *non-restrictive* relative clauses with intonation and corresponding punctuation. Restrictive clauses serve to identify the noun being referred to by adding essential identifying information; they are spoken together with the preceding noun without a pause or a change in pitch and thus in writing are not set off with commas: *The man who came yesterday is sitting over there, the car that I sold him was stolen last week*. Non-restrictive clauses add supplemental information about a noun that is already sufficiently identified; they are set off with commas and in speech are set off with a slight pause and a dip in pitch: *My friend Bill, who was in the army when he learned it, speaks Chinese very well*. (Note that in written English, restrictive clauses require *that* and non-restrictive clauses *which*.) Tajiki distinguishes restrictive and non-restrictive clauses grammatically: Nouns modified by restrictive clauses take the clitic **-e** (which in this construction does *not* indicate indefiniteness), while nouns modified by non-restrictive clauses do not.

Марде, ки дирӯз дидем, дар он ҷо аст,
'The man we saw yesterday is over there.' *(restrictive)*
Он мард, ки дирӯз дидем, дар он ҷо аст,
'That man, the one we saw yesterday, is over there.' *(non-restrictive)*

Tajiki has two kinds of non-restrictive relative clauses, depending on the definiteness of the noun. A non-restrictive clause modifying a definite noun is like the English case; the clause adds further information about a noun whose identity is already known from the sentence and from context. Also, a non-restrictive clause can modify an indefinite noun (which would not be indicated by **-e** but rather by words like **як/ягон**), in which case the entire noun phrase is generic and indicates every person, place, or thing named by that noun.

The simplest cases are when the noun that is being modified is the subject or direct object of both the main sentence and the relative clause. You should take the sentence that is the basis for the relative clause (for example, in *I saw the man who hit you,* 'the man hit you' is the sentence that is relativized) and replace the noun that is going to be modified with **ки**. Thus, 'the man hit you' is **мард туро зад**; since *the man* is the noun being talked about by the relative clause, you should replace **мард** with **ки** to give the relative clause **ки туро зад** '(who) hit you.' Then the noun in the main sentence that is being modified will usually take the clitic **-e**; if it is the direct object of the main sentence it must also take **-po** (which only indicates direct object in this construction) after **-e**. Thus, the main sentence is **Ман мардро дидам,** 'I saw the man,' which becomes **Ман мардеро дидам,** 'I saw the man...' before adding the relative clause. The relative clause can immediately follow either the noun phrase it modifies or the verb of the main sentence; thus:

Ман мардеро дидам, ки дирӯз туро зад,
'I saw the man who hit you.'
Ман мардеро, ки дирӯз туро зад, дидам,
'I saw the man who hit you.'

Note that grammatically the noun being modified by a relative clause is treated as *formally* definite, so when it serves as the direct object of the main sentence it must take **-po**. To make it indefinite in sense (for example, *I saw a man/some people who used to work here*) you can use **як/ягон**:

Ман як мардеро дидам, ки дар ин чо кор мекард,
'I saw a man who used to work here.'

When the noun being modified is the object of a preposition in either the dependent or the independent sentence, its place is filled in the dependent sentence by **ӯ**.

Ман мардеро дидам, ки аз ӯ китобро гирифта будӣ,
'I saw the man from whom you got the book.'
Ман китобро ба марде додам, ки онро аз ӯ гирифта будӣ,
'I gave the book to the man from whom you had taken it.'

In addition, if the noun being modified is the direct object of the relative clause, it is possible to indicate it explicitly with the resumptive pronoun *ӯ* just discussed; that is, one can say the equivalent of *I saw the man whom you hit him*: **Ман мардеро дидам, ки ту ӯро зада будӣ**. This occurs mostly in colloquial speech as a way to keep the reference clear when there are many words between the modified noun and the relative clause.

5. Correlative clauses

Correlative clauses are used to indicate the extent to which something holds true; in English they are used in conjunction with the words *so* or *such*: *He was so hungry that he ate three plates of pilaf, she was such a poor loser that she tossed the board aside and stormed out of the room, he was such a man as to laugh/as would laugh at the merest hint of danger*. *So* modifies an adjective (and thus is an adverb) and *such* a noun phrase (and thus is an adjective); *that* is usually used to introduce an *actual* condition, action or event (the actuality is shown with a verb in the indicative), while *as* with an infinitive or a conditional (indicated by *would*) is used to indicate a general quality or tendency. (In traditional English grammar these are not called "correlative clauses," but instead would be called *emphatic so with that-clauses*.)

Correlative clauses are formed somewhat more simply in Tajiki, which makes no distinction between adjectival *such* and adverbial *so*; both functions are filled by **чунон** 'like that; such, so,' which structurally forms a non-restrictive subordinate clause with the noun or adjective it modifies (that is, the indefinite clitic **-e** is not added to the noun phrase). A general quality or tendency is shown by using the past imperfect tense in the subordinate clause:

Ончунон гушна буд, ки ба хӯрдани гӯсфанд тайёр буд,
'He was so hungry that he was ready to eat a whole sheep.'
Ончунон марди хашмгин аст, ки ба ҳама дод мезанад,
'He's such an angry man that he would yell at everyone.'

A similar construction is *the more...the more...*, as in *The more I study Tajiki, the more I like it.* Such sentences are constructed in Tajiki with the adverbs **ҳар қадар ки...ҳамон қадар**: **Ҳар қадар ки забони тоҷикиро омӯзам, он ба ман ҳамон қадар маъқул аст**, 'The more I study Tajiki, the more I like it.'

6. Subordinate clauses

a. Subordinate clauses of time. Subordinate clauses of time are clauses like *when he saw me, after I went home, before we ate, until I met her,* and *while I was sleeping.* In Tajiki these clauses are generally formed by making the subordinate sentence a relative clause modifying **вақт** 'time' or **он** 'that (time).' **Вақт** is used for *when*; these clauses do not need to be introduced by a preposition, and thus have the structure 'the time that...' Thus, to say *When I saw him*, start with the basic sentence *I saw him* and form the relative clause *the time that I saw him*:

Ман ӯро дидам > Вақте ки ман ӯро дидам, 'When I saw him...'

All subordinate clauses are set off from the main clause by a comma.

Вақте ки вай маро дид, ман сайругашт карда истода будам,
'When he saw me, I was taking a stroll.'

There is no distinct preposition to indicate 'while'; instead, the dependent sentence is put in a **вақт** clause and the verb takes a continuous tense. Thus, in Tajiki *while I slept* is literally *when I was sleeping*.

Вақте ки ман хобида истода будам, борон борид,
'It rained while I was sleeping.'

Most other subordinate clauses of time are formed from a compound preposition containing **аз** 'from' followed by **он ки**. (There is no comma before **ки** because **он ки** constitutes a single unit spoken without a pause or a change in intonation.) The prepositions for *before* are **пеш аз** (Persian) and **қабл аз** (Arabic), and for *after* are **пас аз** (Persian) and **баъд аз** (Arabic); both Persian and Arabic prepositions are common in all levels of Tajiki speech, but **қабл** and **пас** are more literary. So, to say *after I went* *home*, start with the basic sentence *I went home* and add the appropriate preposition followed by **он ки**.

> **Ман ба хона рафтам**, 'I went home.'
> **баъд/пас аз он ки ман ба хона рафтам**, 'After I went home...'

Thus:

> **Баъд аз он ки туро дидам, хоҳарам ба ман номаатро дод**,
> 'After I saw you my sister gave me your letter.'
> **Пеш аз он ки хӯрок хӯрем, мо дар бораи ту гап задем**,
> 'Before we ate we chatted about you.'

There are two ways to say 'until,' **то он вақте ки** and **то даме ки**.

> **То он вақте ки ту дар ин ҷо ҳастӣ, ҳама кор вайрон аст**,
> 'Until you are here, everything's a disaster.'
> **То даме ки Фирӯз ба ин ҷо мерасад, бояд ин дар бораи ин масъала гап назанем**,
> 'Until Firuz gets here, we shouldn't talk this matter.'

To say 'at the same time that, just as, right as,' use the conjunction **ҳамин ки**. In this case the first action cannot be ongoing but instead must just have finished when the second occurs.

> **Ҳамин ки ман хобидаам, ту дарро тақ-тақ кардай**,
> 'Right as I fell asleep, you knocked on the door.'
> *(Indicating that someone told me about it or that I figured it out from the circumstances, hence the past perfect.)*

> **Ҳамин ки ман хобидам, ту дарро тақ-тақ кардӣ**,
> 'Right as I fell asleep, you knocked on the door.' *(Indicating that I know this from my own experience, hence the simple past.)*

Note that in addition to the conjunctions above, **ки** is sometimes used to introduce subordinate clauses of all kinds; this is similar to the use of 'that' in such sentences as *He left for London, that he might find a living.* Except for object clauses, this use is highly literary (just as it is in the English sentence above) and will not be encountered in spoken Tajiki.

The following tables summarize the different clauses of time.

When Вақте ки	• Вақте ки ман бо телефон гап зада истода будам, модарам аз кор омад. • Вақте ки ӯ занг зад, Ситора хӯрокашро хӯрда истода буд. • Вақте ки ман косаю табақ мешустам, духтарам китоб мехонд. • Вақте ки ба бозор меравам, хурсанд мешавам. • Вақте ки ман ба бозор меравам, дӯстонамро мебинам. • Вақте ки ман ба бозор равам, ба ту тарбуз мехарам.	**Вақте ки** means 'at that moment, at that time, etc.' Notice the different tenses used in relation to the *when*-clause. It is important to remember that **вақте ки** takes either the simple past, past narrative, past continuous or the present — the dependent clause changes tense in relation to the *when*-clause. If the *when*-clause is conditional or indicates uncertainty, its main verb is in the subjunctive.
Before Пеш аз он/ ин ки	• Пеш аз он ки ба Тоҷикистон равам, китобҳоямро фиристодам. • Модарам, пеш аз он ки ба кор равад, ҳамеша ноништа мекунад.	**Пеш аз он ки** and **Пеш аз ин ки** mean 'before.' These conjunctions are always followed by the present subjunctive, regardless of the tense of the main clause.
After Пас аз он ки Баъд аз он ки	• Пас аз он ки (Баъд аз он ки) вай ба Амрико омадааст, дӯсти наздикашро вохӯрдааст. • Баъд аз он ки ба Амрико омада будааст, ба Канада рафтааст • Баъд аз он ки ӯ ба хонааш меравад, ба ман занг мезанад.	**Баъд/пас он ки** means 'after that moment,' therefore the action in its clause always precedes the action of the main clause. Depending on the meaning, the verb of the main clause can take any tenses except the continuous ones.

| Until, till
То даме ки
То замоне ки	• То даме ки кор наёбам, мушкил боқӣ мемонад.	'Until' and 'till' express 'up to that time.' Either the simple present or simple past is used with тодаме ки/то замоне ки.
As soon as
Ҳамин ки	• Ҳамин ки ӯ ба хулосае ояд, ба мо маълум мекунад.	Ҳамин ки means 'immediately after something happens.' 'As soon as' is very similar to 'when' and emphasizes that the event will occur immediately after the other. The simple present is usually used for future events, although the present perfect can also be used.
Whenever, every time
Ҳар боре ки	• Ҳар боре ки ӯ моро хабар гирад, мо якҷоя ба тарабхона меравем.	Ҳар боре ки means 'each time something happens.' The simple present (or the simple past) is used because 'whenever' and 'every time' already expresses habitual action.

b. Subordinate clauses of place. Subordinate clauses of place are those like *We went <u>where you had gone</u>*. Because all locations are indicated in Tajiki by prepositional phrases containing nouns of location, subordinate clauses of place are simply indicated by prepositional phrases containing **он ҷо** 'place' (or another noun like **шаҳр** 'city') with a relative clause for the subordinated clause; often, however, there is no need for the resumptive phrase in the subordinate clause, as it would sound too formal or heavy:

Мо ба он ҷое рафтем, ки шумо (аз он ҷо) омада будед,
'We went (to the place) where you came from.'

c. Subordinate clauses of reason and purpose. To tell why someone did something, subordinate clauses of reason or cause (introduced by such conjunctions as *because, since, for,* and *as*) and purpose (indicated by *to, in order to, so as to,* and so on) are used. The major difference between the two is that reasons refer to *actual* events or circumstances while purposes indicate *potential* events or circumstances that the subject intends to bring about; thus, purpose clauses require a subjunctive and reason clauses do not.

The most common subordinate conjunctions of reason in Tajiki are **чунки, зеро (ки),** and **аз сабаби он ки,** all meaning 'because, since.' Another conjunction, **азбаски,** is highly literary. Subordinate clauses beginning with **чунки** and **зеро (ки)** must *follow* the main clause, while those beginning with **аз сабаби он ки** and **азбаски** must *precede* it.

> **Мо пагоҳ ба хонаи шумо рафта наметавонем, чунки соати 4 маҷлис дорем,** 'We are not able to go to your house tomorrow because we have a meeting at four o'clock.'
> **Дирӯз ман ба донишгоҳ нарафтам, зеро модарам бемор буд,** 'I didn't go to university yesterday because my mother was sick.'
> **Азбаски бори аввал ба Душанбе омада буд, ҳанӯз ҳеҷ ҷойро намедонист,** 'Because it was his first time in Dushanbe, he didn't know any places yet.'
> **Ман суханҳои ӯро нафаҳмидам, барои он ки забони тоҷикиро нағз намедонам,** 'I didn't understand what he said because I don't know Tajiki well.'

The most common subordinating conjunctions of purpose are **барои он ки, то,** and **то (он) ки,** all meaning 'in order to, so as to'; only **барои он ки** is common in spoken Tajiki. As mentioned above, these conjunctions require the verb in the subordinate clause to be in the subjunctive. Subordinate clauses of purpose can occur either before or after the main clause.

> **Барои он ки нағз хобам, ман қаҳва нанӯшидам,** 'So's to sleep well, I didn't drink coffee.'
> **Ман қаҳва нанӯшидам, барои он ки нағз хобам,** 'So that I would sleep well, I didn't drink coffee.'
> **Вай ба Душанбе меравад, то ҳамсарашро бинад,** 'He's going to Dushanbe to meet (see) his wife.'
> (or 'She's going to Dushanbe to see her husband.')

То ки забони русиро нағз омӯзам, ман ба Маскав меравам,
'I'm going to study in Moscow in order to learn Russian well.'
Модар болои писарашро бо кӯрпа пӯшид, то ки касал нашавад,
'The mother laid a quilt over her son so that he wouldn't become ill.'
Барои он ки аз ман наранҷад, ба ӯ чизе нагуфтам,
'In order not to offend him, I didn't say anything to him.'

Remember that in highly literary Tajiki subordinate clauses of reason and purpose can also be introduced by the all-purpose conjunction **ки** 'that.' When followed by a clause with a verb in the subjunctive, this often indicates a purpose clause; otherwise, its sense is determined by context.

Пагоҳӣ Гулноз омад, ки туро бинад,
'Gulnoz came to see you in the morning.'
Ин гапро ба падарат нагӯй, ки туро ҷанг мекунад,
'Don't tell your father this, because/or he'll tell you off.'

Subordinate clauses of cause and purpose are also frequently used by themselves in questions and answers:

- **Ту чаро ба кор нарафтӣ?** 'Why didn't you go to work?'
- **Барои ин ки бемор будам,** 'Because I was ill.'
- **Шумо барои чӣ омадед?** 'Why have you come?'
- **Барои он ки Шуморо бинам,** 'To see you.'
- **Чаро падарат кор намекунад?** 'Why doesn't your father work?'
- **Чунки ҳанӯз ягон кори нағз наёфтааст,**
  'Because he hasn't found any good work yet.'

7. Conditional sentences

Conditional sentences are those like *If he wants to sleep, then he shouldn't drink coffee this late,* in which one action or state occurs when a condition holds or is fulfilled. The condition, called the *protasis*, is usually indicated in English with an *if*-clause; the action or state dependent on the condition, called the *apodosis*, is often indicated with a *then*-clause. The Tajiki word for *if* is **агар**, which is always the first word in the protasis when it occurs. (It is possible to omit **агар** in certain types of conditional sentences just as in English: *Were he here, he'd tell us.* It is more frequently omitted in Tajiki than in English.) There is no word for *then* in Tajiki; that is, the apodosis is not specially marked. The protasis usually comes first in a Tajiki sentence.

a. The different kinds of conditional sentences. There are several kinds of conditional sentences, each of which is distinguished by the tense of the verb in both English and Tajiki. The basic distinction is between counterfactuals and possible conditionals. Counterfactuals describe situations that are impossible or contrary to fact, while possible conditionals describe situations that are known to be true or that might be true (however doubtful). The difference between the two can be seen in the following pair of sentences.

> *If I was a total cad, I apologize.* (Possible conditional)
> *If I were a total cad, I'd never apologize.* (Counterfactual)

The other important distinction common to English and Tajiki is between past and present-future conditionals. In English possible conditionals, the verb in the protasis is indicative, not subjunctive; it is in a past tense for past conditionals and the present for present or future conditionals.

> *If he went to the store, he bought food.* (Past possible)
> *If he's sick, he shouldn't be in school.* (Present possible)
> *If he goes to the store, tell him to buy apples.* (Future possible)

In English counterfactuals, the protasis takes the subjunctive for present or future and the past perfect for past; the apodosis takes the past or present conditional depending on tense.

> *If Bill were happy, he wouldn't be (wouldn't have been) such a killjoy.* (Present counterfactual)
> *If you hadn't left the meat out, the cat wouldn't have eaten it/it would still be fresh.* (Past counterfactual)

b. Tajiki possible conditionals. Possible conditionals are more complex in Tajiki than in English, for in Tajiki you must distinguish between *actual* and *doubtful* conditionals. Actual conditionals are those in which the condition is known to be true, while for doubtful conditionals the condition might be true or false. In actual conditionals in

Tajiki, the verb in the protasis must be in the present-future tense. (Often an actual conditional is replaced by a subordinate clause of time: 'When you go...' instead of 'If you go.')

Агар ту меравӣ, ман бо ту меравам, 'If you go, I'll go with you.'
(The speaker knows for certain that the other person is going.)

In present doubtful conditionals the verb in the protasis must be in either the present subjunctive or the simple past tense. Use of the subjunctive indicates greater doubt that the event will actually come about; if the verb is in the simple past tense, **агар** is best translated *when*.

Агар ту равӣ, ба ман занг зан, 'If you go, give me a call.'
(The present subjunctive implies that there is a distinct possibility that the person will not go.)
Агар ту рафтӣ, ба ман занг зан,
'When you go, give me a call.' *(The simple past implies that it is quite likely that the person will go; often* **вақте ки рафтӣ...** *is used instead.)*
Агар имрӯз борон наборад, барои истироҳат ба дараи Варзоб меравем, 'If it doesn't rain today, we're going to go take a rest at Varzob Gorge.'
Агар бародарат биёяд, гӯй ки маро бинад,
'If your brother comes, tell him to see me.'

In past doubtful conditionals the verb in the protasis takes the *perfect subjunctive*, which is composed of the past participle of the main verb and the auxiliary subjunctive stem **бош**: **карда бошам** 'that I did.'

Агар вай ба хона рафта бошад, мо ба вай занг зада метавонем, 'If he went home, we can call him.'

The difference between actual and doubtful conditionals can be shown in English by using *since* instead of *if*; thus, in the sentence *If you're leaving, could you return this to John?*, you can replace *if* with *since* if you know that the person will definitely leave in the near future: **Агар ту меравӣ, ман бо ту меравам** can be translated as 'Since you're going, I'll go with you.' On the other hand, if there is some doubt that the person will leave, you must use *if*. Thus, if you are unsure whether a sentence is an actual or a doubtful conditional, change *if* to *since* in the English sentence; if the sense of the sentence is unchanged, then it is an actual conditional. In general doubtful conditionals are much more common than actual conditionals.

c. Tajiki counterfactuals. Counterfactuals are formed by putting the verbs in both the protasis and the apodosis in the past imperfect tense. (In such sentences **будан** and **доштан** can take the prefix **ме-**, which here serves to indicate the counterfactual, though **будан** is often replaced by **шудан** in such sentences.) Thus, Tajiki counterfactual sentences do not show tense, which is determined by context. However, since past counterfactuals are overwhelmingly more common than present counterfactuals, this is not a major difficulty.

Агар вай ба хонаяш мерафт, мо вайро медидем,
'If he had gone home, we would have seen him.'
Агар вай дар хона мебуд/мешуд, мо вайро медидем,
'If he had been at home, we would have seen him; if he were at home, we would see him.'

Агар вай дар хона мебуд/мешуд, ман худам аз вай мепурсидам,
'If he had been at home, I would have asked him myself.'
Агар ман мошин медоштам, аз ҳама шодтар мебудам/ мешудам,
'If I had had a car, I would have been the happiest fellow in the world.'

In literary language, especially in poetry, two abbreviated forms of **агар** are also used, **гар** and **ар**:

Гар бар сари нафси худ амирӣ, мардӣ,
Бар кӯру кар ар нукта нагирӣ, мардӣ.
Мардӣ набувад фитодаро пой задан,
Гар дасти фитодае бигирӣ, мардӣ. (Рӯдакӣ)

If you would covet being an emir, you are really a man,
If you don't mock the blind and deaf, you are really a man.
You have no courage if you kick a man when he's down,
If you take the hand of such a man, you are really a man. (Rudaki)

In addition to **агар**, there are two other indicators of a condition, **ба шарте ки** 'on condition that, so long as' and **то**, here meaning 'if.'

Ман ин корро мекунам, ба шарте ки Шумо розӣ бошед, 'I'm going to do this job, on condition that you agree.'
Шумо сиҳат мешавед, ба шарте ки ҳамаи гуфтаҳои духтурро иҷро кунед, 'You'll get better so long as you do everything the doctor said.'
То бисёр такрор накунӣ, забони тоҷикиро ёд намегирӣ, 'If you don't repeat it many times, you won't learn Tajiki.'

Tajiki-English Glossary

All Tajiki words used in this book are included below; however, only the meanings relevant to their occurrence in the book are included. The following abbreviations are used:

(N)	northern dialect
adj.	adjective
adv.	adverb
adv.phr.	adverbial phrase
c.prep.	compound preposition (when the noun is used only with the given simple preposition)
*c.prep.	noun used to form a compound preposition (may be preceded by **дар, ба**, or **аз** to indicate location or motion towards or away from; must take izofat)
coll.	colloquial
conj.	conjunction
interj.	interjection
intr.	intransitive
intro.part.	introductory particle
intro.phr.	introductory phrase
lit.	literary
n.	noun; special plural forms given in parentheses
n.phr.	noun phrase
n.prep.	nominal preposition
num.	numeral
part.	particle
pl	plural
prep.	other lexical item corresponding to an English preposition
pron.	pronoun
s.prep.	simple preposition
sg	singular
trans.	transitive
v.	verb; present stem given after infinitive (except for compound verbs)

- А -

абр *n.* cloud
абрӯ *n.* eyebrow
абрӯкамон *adj.* with arched brows
аввал(ин) *adj.* first
август *n.* August
агар *conj.* if (*with subjunctive, simple past, or past imperfect*), since (*with present-future*)
адаб *n.* politeness, civility; culture, civilization
адабиёт *n.* literature
аз *s.prep.* from
аз байни *c.prep.* through
аз миёни *c.prep.* through
аз пеш *adv.* than before, than ever
аз роҳи *c.prep.* via
аз сабаби он ки *conj.* because, since
аз тарафи *c.prep.* by (*indicating the agent in passive sentences*)
аз тариқи *c.prep.* via
аз як тараф/сӯ...аз тарафи/ сӯйи дигар *intro.phr.* on the one hand...on the other
азбаски *conj.* because, since
ако *n.* elder brother
аксаран *adv.* mostly, generally
ақалан *adv.* at least
ақл *n.* reason, intellect
алқисса *conj.* in conclusion
аллакай *adv.* already
ало *interj.* hello, hey
алҳол *adv.* now
амир *n.* emir, prince
аммо *conj.* but
Амрико *n.* America, US
амрикойӣ *adj.* American
ана *pron.* that one there
андак *adv.* a little
анор *n.* pomegranate
апа *n.* older sister
апрел *n.* April
аскар *n.* soldier
асп *n.* horse
аспбон *n.* stable-man
атроф *n.* sides; *c.prep.* around
афсӯс *interj.* alas
афтидан/афт *v.* to fall
афтон *adv.* falling
ахбор *n.* news
ахтар *n.* star
аҳром *n.* pyramid

- Б -

ба *s.prep.* to, towards
ба гӯш расидан/рас *v.* to be heard/audible
бадин сон *intro.phr.* thus (= ин тавр)
ба замми ин *intro.phr.* moreover, in addition (*formal*, = идова ба ин)
ба ибораи дигар *intro.phr.* that is to say
ба мисли *c.prep.* like
ба муқобили *c.prep.* against
ба ростӣ *intro.phr.* indeed (= дар воқеъ, ҳақиқатан)
ба сари...дард задан/зан *v.* to give a headache to
ба ҳамин тариқ *intro.phr.* so, in the same way (= ҳамин тавр)

ба чашм/гӯш расидан *v.* to be visible/audible
ба ҷои *prep.* instead of
ба ҷояш *adv.* instead
ба ҷуз *s.prep.* except for
ба шарте ки *conj.* on condition that, so long as
бад *adj.* bad
бадбахтона *intro.part.* unfortunately
бадтар *adj.* worse
байн **c.prep.* between
баланд *adj.* tall
бале *interj.* yes (= **оре, ҳа**)
банд *adj.* busy, bound
банда *n.* slave
бандча *n.* bundle
бар *s.prep.* over
бар зидди *c.prep.* against
барг *n.* leaf
баргаштан/баргард *v.* to return (*intr.*)
баробар *adj.* equal
бародар *n.* brother
барои *s.prep.* for
барои ҳамин/ҳамон *intro.phr.* therefore
баромадан/баро *v.* to come out
барф *n.* snow
бастан/банд *v.* to tie, bind
баҳор *n.* spring (*season*)
баҳс кардан *v.* to discuss
бача *n.* child
баъд *n.prep.* after; *adv.* later
баъд аз *n.prep.* after
баъзан *adv.* now and then, on occasion, sometimes
баъзе *pron.* some, a few
бе *s.prep.* without
беақл *adj.* foolish

бегоҳ *n.* evening
бегоҳӣ *adv.* in the evening
бегуноҳ *adj.* sinless
бедил *adj.* heartless, ruthless; cowardly
беихтиёр *adj.* unwillingly
бемазза *adj.* tasteless, bland
бемор *adj.* sick
бемористон *n.* hospital
берун **c.prep.* outside
бесавод *adj.* illiterate
беҳ *adj.* good (*predicative use only*)
беҳин *adj.* best
беҳтар *adj.* better
беҳтар аст *conj.* it is better (that)
беҳтарин *adj.* best
бечора *adj.* poor
беш *adv.* more
беш аз пеш *adv.* more than ever
бешарм *adj.* shameless
бештар *adj.* more
бештарин *adj.* most
бешубҳа *adv.* undoubtedly
бигзор *conj.* let it be that, allow
биниш *n.* sight
бино *adj.* capable of seeing
бинобар ин *intro.part.* thus (*because of this*)
бирён *adj.* fried
биринҷ *n.* rice
бисёр *adv., adj.* many, much
бисёрошёна *adj.* multi-storey
бист *num.* twenty
бо *s.prep.* with
бо вуҷуди ин/он *intro.phr.* however, nonetheless
бо забони тоҷикӣ *adv.phr.* in Tajiki
боадаб *adj.* polite
боақл *adj.* wise

бобо *n.* grandfather, old man
боғ *n.* garden
бод *n.* wind
боз *adv.* still; again
боз кардан *v.* to open (*trans.*)
боз як чизи дигар *n.phr.* something else (*in addition*)
бозгаштан/бозгард *v.* to return, come back (*intr.*)
бозикунон *adv.* playfully
бозингар *n.* player, sportsman
бозор *n.* bazaar, market
боистеъдод *adj.* talented
бой *adj.* rich
боло **c.prep.* over, above
бом *n.* roof
бомазза *adj.* delicious
бомаърифат *adj.* intelligent
бону *n.* lady
бор *n.* time, occasion
боракалло *interj.* good job!
боридан/бор *v.* to fall (*of precipitation*)
борон *n.* rain
борон боридан *v.* to rain
бороні *adj.* rainy
ботантана *adj.* festive
бофаҳм *adj.* wise
бояд *adv.* must
бубин *interj.* see here
будан/бош *v.* to be (*provides past tense for the personal possessive markers and* **ҳаст**)
бузкашй *n.* buzkashi (*sport in which riders on horseback compete to drag a goat carcass to a goal*)
бузург *adj.* high
бузургӣ *n.* height
бурдан/бар *v.* to carry
бӯй *n.* smell
бӯй кардан *v.* to smell (*trans.*)
бӯйнок *adj.* smelly, stinking
бо *s.prep.* with

- В -

ва *conj.* and
ваё *pron.* 3rd *pl:* they, them (*coll. for* **вайҳо**)
вазифаи хонагӣ *n.* homework
вазнин *adj.* serious
вай *pron.* 3rd *sg:* he/him, she/her, it
вайҳо *pron.* 3rd *pl:* they, them (= **ваё**)
вақт *n.* time
вақте ки *conj.* when
вале *conj.* but
Ватан *n.* homeland, motherland
вафот *n.* death
вафот кардан *v.* to die, perish
ветеран *n.* army veteran
водӣ *n.* valley
воқеа *n.* event
волид *n.* parent
волидайн *n.* both parents
ворид *n.* entering, entry, entrance
воридот *n.* imports
вохӯрдан/вохӯр *v.* to meet, come across

- Г -

газидан/газ *v.* to bite
гап *n.* talk, words
гап задан *v.* to chat, talk

гапзанӣ *n.* talking
гардидан/гард *v.* to wander
гардиш кардан *v.* to take a walk
гарм *adj.* hot
гарм кардан *v.* to warm up (*trans.*)
гарм шудан *v.* to become warm
гаштан/гард *v.* to turn, spin (*intr.*)
гирён *adv.* crying, weeping
гиристан/(гирй) *v.* to cry, weep (*forms with present stem are rare and usually replaced by* **гиря кардан**)
гирифтан/гир *v.* to take, obtain, get, catch
гиро *adj.* attractive
гиря *n.* crying, weeping
гиря кардан *v.* to cry, weep
гов *n.* cow
гоҳ-гоҳ *adv.* sometimes
гузаронидан/гузарон *v.* to celebrate
гузарондан/гузарон *v.* to pass (*trans.*), spend (*time*)
гузашта *adj.* last (*week, etc.*), past
гузаштан/гузар *v.* to cross (**аз** across), to pass (*trans.*)
гул *n.* flower, rose
гум кардан *v.* to lose (*trans.*)
гум шудан *v.* to get/become lost
гуноҳ *n.* sin
гурба *n.* cat
гурбача *n.* kitten
гурусна *adj.* hungry
гуфтан/гӯ(й) *v.* to say
гуфтугӯй *n.* telling
гӯё *adj.* capable of speech
гӯё ки *conj.* as if
гӯсфанд *n.* sheep
гӯш *n.* ear
гӯш кардан *v.* to listen (*trans.* with **ба**; *intr.* for)
гӯшак *n.* telephone receiver
гӯшт *n.* meat

- F -

ғайри *s.prep.* except
ғам *n.* grief, sorrow
ғамгин *adj.* sorrowful, sad
ғарбиёна *adj.* western, occidental
ғарбӣ *adj.* western, from the west

- Д -

давидан/дав *v.* to run (*intr.*)
даводав *n.* fuss, bustle
далерона *adv.* bravely
дам кардан *v.* to make (*tea, coffee*)
даме ки *conj.* when
дар 1. *s.prep.* in, at 2. *n.* door
дар баробари ин/он *intro. phr.* besides (*indicating similarity; see* **новобаста ба ин/он**)
дар воқеъ *intro. phr.* indeed (= **ба ростӣ, ҳақиқатан**)
дар ин сурат *intro.phr.* in this case
дар муқоиса *intro.phr.* in contrast
дар натиҷа *intro.phr.* as a result
дар он сурат *intro.phr.* in

that case
дар ҳақиқат *intro.phr.* in fact
дара *n.* gorge
дарахт *n.* tree
дарахтзор *n.* arbor, orchard
дараҷа *n.* degree (*of temperature*)
даргирифтан/даргир *v.* to catch on fire (*intr.*), come alight
дард *n.* pain
дарднок *adj.* painful
дарё *n.* river
дароз *adj.* long
дароз кашидан/каш *v.* to lie down
даромадан/даро *v.* to come in
даррав *adv.* immediately
дарс *n.* lesson, class
дарун **c.prep.* inside
дарҳол *adv.* immediately
даст *n.* hand
даста *n.* bunch, group, handle
даста-даста *adv.* in groups
дасти рост **c.prep.* right (side) of
дасти чап **c.prep.* left (side) of
даҳ *num.* ten
даъват кардан *v.* to invite (**ба** to)
даъват шудан *v.* to be invited (**ба** to)
декабр *n.* December
дер *adj.* late
дер кардан *v.* to be late (**ба** to)
деҳа *n.* village
диван *n.* sofa
дигар *adj.* other
дидан/бин *v.* to see

дил *n.* heart
дина *adv.* yesterday
дирӯз *adv.* yesterday
дифоъ кардан *v.* to defend
дишаб *adv.* last night
дод задан *v.* to yell, shout (**ба** at)
додан/диҳ (деҳ) *v.* to give
додар *n.* younger brother
доллар *n.* dollar
дона *n. classifier for things*
донистан/дон *v.* to know
дониш *n.* knowledge
дониш омӯхтан *v.* to learn
донишгоҳ *n.* university
донишманд *adj.* wise, learned
донишҷӯ *n.* university student
доно *adj.* wise
доро *adj.* rich; having
доштан/дор *v.* to have
ду *num.* two
ду-ду *adv.* in pairs, by pairs
дувоздаҳ *num.* twelve
дузд *n.* thief
дунё *n.* world
дуо хондан *v.* to pray, recite a prayer
дур *adj.* far, distant
дуруст *adj.* correct
дусола *adj.* two-year-old
духтар *n.* daughter, girl
духтур *n.* doctor
дучарха *n.* bicycle
душанбе *n.* Monday
дӯст доштан *v.* to like
дӯстдошта *adj.* favorite
дӯхтан/дӯз *v.* to sew

- Е -

елим *n.* glue, paste

- Ё -

ё *conj.* or
ё...ё *conj.* either...or
ё (ин) ки *conj.* or else
ёд гирифтан/гир *v.* learn (*by heart*)
ёздаҳ *num.* eleven
ёқут *n.* ruby
ёр *n.* sweetheart, beloved
ёфтан/ёб *v.* to find

- З -

забон *n.* tongue, language
задан/зан *v.* to hit
зан *n.* woman
занг задан *v.* to call by phone (*intr., uses* **ба**)
занона *adj.* women's, of/for women
зарар дидан *v.* to be injured, suffer harm
заҳмат *n.* burden
зебо *adj.* beautiful
зер *c.prep.* under, below
зеро (ки) *conj.* because
зид *adj.* contrary
зиёд *adj.* (a great) many
зиндагӣ *n.* life
зиндагӣ кардан *v.* to inhabit, live (*in a place*)
зодрӯз *n.* birthday
зону *n.* knee
зуд *adv.* soon
зуд-зуд *adv.* often

- И -

илова ба ин *intro.phr.* moreover, in addition (= **ба замми ин**)
иқлим *n.* climate
иқтисод *n.* economy
иқтисодчӣ *n.* economist
имрӯз *adv.* today
имсол *adv.* this year
имтиҳон *n.* test, exam
имшаб *adv.* tonight
ин *pron., adj.* this
ин қадар *adv.* this much
ин тавр *intro.phr.* thus, hence (= **ба дин сон**)
ин хел *adv.* this way
ин ҷо *n.* here
инчунин *adj.* like this; *intro. part.* also
иншо *n.* essay, composition
истеъдод *n.* talent, ability
истироҳат *n.* rest
истодан/ист(о) *v.* to stand, stay, stop (*intr.*)
иттилоот *n.* information
иттилоъ *n.* piece of information
иҷро кардан *v.* to fulfill, do (*homework, assignment*), follow (*instructions*)
ишқ *n.* love
июл *n.* July
июн *n.* June

- К -

кабуд *adj.* blue
кадом *adj.* which?
кадомин *adj.* which?
кай *adv.* when?

калон *adj.* large
кам *adj., adv.* few, little
камакак *adv.* very little
камбағал *adj.* poor
каме *adv.* a little
канӣ *adv.* where? (*location*)
кар *adj.* deaf
кардан/кун *v.* to do
Карочӣ *n.* Karachi
касал *adj.* ill
кашидан *v.* to smoke (*tobacco*)
ки *conj.* that (*to mark relative clauses*)
кило *n.* kilogram
километр *n.* kilometer
ким-кадом *adj.* some such
ким-кӣ *pron.* someone
ким-чӣ *pron.* something
кино *n.* movie
китоб *n.* book
китф *n.* shoulder
кӣ *pron.* who?
комилан *adv.* completely
кор *n.* work, job
кор кардан *v.* to work
корд *n.* knife
коса *n.* cup
кофтан/коб *v.* to look for
кошкӣ *conj.* would that
курсича *n.* stool
курсӣ *n.* chair
куҷо *n.* where?
кушодан/кушо *v.* to open
куштан/куш *v.* to kill
кӯдак *n.* child (= **бала, бача**)
кӯдакӣ *n.* childhood
кӯй *n.* house (*literary*)
кӯр *adj.* blind
кӯрпа *n.* quilt
кӯҳ *n.* mountain

кӯҳистонӣ *n.* mountain dweller
кӯҳсор *n.* mountain

- Қ -

қабл аз *n.prep.* before
қадбаланд *adj.* tall (*of person*)
қалам *n.* pencil
қанд *n.* sweets
қафо *n.* back; *c.prep.* behind
қаҳва *n.* coffee
қиматтар *adj.* expensive
қулай *adj.* comfortable, convenient
қуфл *n.* lock
қуфл кардан *v.* to lock (*trans.*)
қуфл шудан *v.* to be locked

- Л -

лаб *n.* lip; edge; *c.prep.* right beside, next to
лағмон *n.* laghman (*dish with meat, noodles, and various peppers*)
лекин *conj.* however
литр *n.* liter
лоақал *adv.* at least
лозим аст *conj.* it is necessary (that)
лола *n.* tulip
лолазор *n.* tulip garden

- М -

мабодо *conj.* beware, I fear
мағоза *n.* store
мазза *n.* taste
май *n.* May
майлаш *interj.* okay
мактаб (**макотиб**) *n.* school

мактуб *n.* letter (*mail*)
ман *pron.* 1ˢᵗ *sg:* I, me, etc.
мана *pron.* this one here
мард *n.* man
мардикор *n.* worker
мардона *adj.* men's, for men
мардум *n.* people
маротиба *n.* time, occasion
март *n.* March
масалан *intro.part.* for example, thus (*introducing an example*)
Маскав *n.* Moscow
маҳфил (маҳофил) *n.* club, group
маҷбур будан *conj.* to be compelled to
маҷлис *n.* meeting (*official*)
машғала (машоғил) *n.* noise
маъқул *adj.* interesting
маълум *adj.* clear; *n.* something known
маълумот *n.* information
маъмулан *adv.* usually
маърифат *n.* education
мева *n.* fruit
метр *n.* meter (*unit of length*)
миён **c.prep.* among
миз *n.* table
миллиард *num.* a thousand millions (UK milliard, US billion)
миллион *num.* million
минбаъд *adv.* hereinafter
модар *n.* mother
моён *pron.* 1ˢᵗ *pl:* we, us (N)
монанд ба *prep.* like
мондан/мон *v.* to remain; to put, place
моҳ *n.* month

моҳича *n.* small fish, fry
моҳӣ *n.* fish
мошин *n.* car
мо *pron.* 1ˢᵗ *pl:* we, us, etc.; 1ˢᵗ *sg:* I, me, etc. (N)
муаллим *n.* teacher
мувофиқи *prep.* according to
муғча *n.* bud
мумкин аст *conj.* it is possible (that)
мурдан/мир~мур *v.* to die
мусиқӣ *n.* music
мусофир *n.* passenger, traveler
мӯй *n.* hair
мӯйсафед *n.* old man

- **Н** -

набера *n.* grandchild
набошад *conj.* if so
нав *adj.* new
навад *num.* ninety
навакак *adv.* just now, recently
навиштан/навис *v.* to write
навиштаҷот *n.* compositions, writings, oeuvre
навохтан/навоз *v.* to play (*an instrument*)
Наврӯз *n.* Navruz (*the Persian New Year*)
нағз *adj.* good (= **хуб**)
назд **c.prep.* near
наздик *n.prep.* near; *adj.* close
нам *n.* moisture
намнок *adj.* humid
намудан/намо *v.* to seem, appear
наргис *n.* narcissus flower
насим *n.* feeling
нафар *n.* classifier for people

нафс *n.* desire, greed
наход (ки) *adv.* really
нахустин *adj.* first
наҳорӣ *n.* breakfast
на...на *conj.* neither...nor
не *interj.* no
нест *v.* is not; there is not (*negative equational and existential verb*)
нигоҳ *n.* sight
нигоҳ кардан *n.* to look at (*trans.*); to watch (*trans. with* **ба**; *intr.* for)
нигоштан/нигор *n.* to write (*for publication*)
низ *adv.* also, too (*literary, follows noun*)
ним *num.* half
нимашаб *adv.* midnight
нисбат ба *prep.* compared to
нисф *num.* half
нисфирӯзӣ *adj.* noontime
ниҳоят *intro.part.* finally (= **охир**)
нишастан/(ни)шин *v.* to sit
нобуд *adj.* gone, absent
новобаста ба *prep.* despite, for all
новобаста ба ин/он *intro.phr.* besides (*indicating contrast; see* **дар баробари ин/он**)
нодон *adj.* stupid
нодонӣ *n.* ignorance, foolishness
нодуруст *adj.* incorrect
нозук *adj.* soft
ноқулай *adj.* uncomfortable
нол *num.* zero (= **сифр**)
нола *v.* groan, lamentation, cry of dismay
нома *n.* letter (*mail*)

нон *n.* bread
нонвой *n.* baker
нопурра *adj.* incomplete
нотарс *adj.* fearless
ноҳост *adv.* suddenly
ноҳия *n.* region
ноябр *n.* November
нуздаҳ *num.* nineteen
нуқра *n.* silver
нӯҳ *num.* nine

- О -

об *n.* water
обо *interj.* uh-oh!
обкаш *n.* water sprinkler
об кардан *v.* to melt (*trans.*)
об шудан *v.* to melt (*intr.*)
овардан/овар~ор *v.* to bring
овехтан/овез *v.* to hang (*trans.*)
овоз *n.* voice, sound
одам *n.* a human
одамон *n.* humans (*pl. of* **одам**), people (*generic*)
одатан *adv.* usually, customarily
оё *part.* yes/no question word
озод *adj.* free (*political*)
оид ба *prep.* about (*concerning*)
ойина *n.* mirror
октябр *n.* October
омадан/о *v.* to come
омӯзиш *n.* training, instruction
омӯхтан/омӯз *v.* to learn, to study
он *pron.* 3rd *sg:* he/him, she/her, it; that; *adj.* that
он қадар *adv.* that much
он хел *adv.* that way

он ҷо *n.* there
онҳо *pron. 3rd pl:* they, them (= **уно**)
ончунин *adj.* like that
оре *interj.* yes (*formal*, = **ҳа, бале**)
осон *adj.* easy
охир(он) *intro.part.* finally (= **ниҳоят**)
оҳанин *adj.* iron, made of iron
оҳиста *adv.* quickly
ошиқ *n.* sweetheart, beloved, lover
ошхона *n.* restaurant
оянда *adj.* next (*week, etc.*); coming

- П -

пагоҳӣ *adv.* in the morning
падар *n.* father
палав/палов *n.* pilaf
панҷ *num.* five
панҷа *n.* the five fingers, hand, paw
панҷоҳ *num.* fifty
панҷшанбе *n.* Thursday
парерсол *adv.* the year before last
парерӯз *adv.* the day before yesterday
парешаб *adv.* two nights ago
паридан/пар *v.* to fly
пас *n.prep.* behind; *adv.* later
пас аз *n.prep.* after
пасин *adj.* last
пасноки *adv.* backwards
пасфардо *adv.* day after tomorrow
пахта *n.* cotton
пахтакор *n.* cotton-grower
пахтачинӣ *n.* picking of cotton
паҳлӯ *n.* side; **c.prep.* beside
пеш *n.* front; *n.prep.* before; *adv.* earlier
пеш аз *n.prep.* before
пешин *n.* noon, early afternoon
пешинӣ *adj.* at noon, in/of the early afternoon; *n.* lunch (*short for* **хӯроки пешинӣ**)
пешпо хӯрдан *v.* to stumble
пешпохӯрон *adv.* stumbling
пиёла *n.* cup, bowl (*for tea, etc.*)
пир *adj.* old
пиразан *n.* old woman
писар *n.* son
поён **c.prep.* under, below, at the base of
поён ёфтан *v.* to come to an end
понздаҳ *num.* fifteen
порина *adv.* last year
порсол *adv.* last year
пул *n.* money
пурра *adj.* complete; *adv.* completely, fully
пурсидан/пурс *v.* to ask (**аз** of)
пухтан/паз *v.* to cook; to ripen
пухтупаз *n.* cooking
пушаймон *adj.* sorry (**аз** for)
пушт **c.prep.* behind
пӯшидан/пӯш *v.* to put on, wear (*clothes*); cover (*trans.*)

- Р -

рабудан/рабо *v.* to seize
радио *n.* radio

раис *n.* head (*of a company or division*), chief, boss
раққоса *n.* female dancer
рақс *n.* dance
рақс кардан *v.* to dance
рақсидан/рақс *v.* to dance
рақскунон *adv.* dancing(ly)
ранг *n.* color
рангин *adj.* colored
ранчидан/ранч *v.* to be offended, take offense (**аз** at)
расидан/рас *v.* to reach (*literal and figurative: maturity*)
расо *adj.* mature, exact
рассом *n.* artist
рафтан/рав *v.* to go
рафтуо *n.* visit
рехтан/рез *v.* to pour
рисола *n.* thesis
розй *adj.* agreed, in agreement
рост *n.* right (*direction*)
рост истодан *v.* to be standing, to stand straight
рох *n.* road
рохравон *adv.* while going
роцеъ ба *prep.* about (*concerning*)
рубъ *num.* quarter
рӯбарӯй *c.prep.* opposite, facing
рӯз *n.* day
рӯзнома *n.* newspaper
рӯзона *adj.* in the daytime, daily
рӯй *n.* face; *c.prep.* on top of
рӯфтан/рӯб *v.* to sweep up

- С -

сабаб *n.* reason
сабз *adj.* green
сабза *n.* green things
сабзавот *n.* vegetables
сабзй *n.* carrot
савдогар *n.* merchant
савод *n.* literacy
саг *n.* dog
сад *num.* hundred
сайёра *n.* planet
сайругашт кардан *v.* to stroll
саломат *adj.* healthy
саломатй *n.* health
санг *n.* stone
сангин *adj.* (of) stone, stony
сар *n.* head, beginning; *classifier for animals*
сар кардан *v.* to start (*trans.*)
сар шудан *v.* to start (*intr.*)
сарват *n.* wealth
сарватманд *adj.* rich
сардард *n.* headache
саросемагй *n.* confusion
сафар кардан *v.* to travel
сафед *adj.* white
сафедй *n.* whiteness; yogurt
сахткор *adj.* hard-working
сахифа *n.* page (*of book*)
сахро *n.* field
се *num.* three
себ *n.* apple
себзор *n.* apple orchard
сездах *num.* thirteen
сентябр *n.* September
сер *adj.* full (*esp. of food*)
сешанбе *n.* Tuesday
сеяк *num.* a third
сигор *n.* cigar

Симурғ *n.* mythical Persian bird of wisdom
син(н) *n.* age
синну сол/синнусол *n.* age
ситора *n.* star
сифр *num.* zero
сиҳат *adj.* recovered, well, better
сй *num.* thirty
соат *n.* clock, hour
содир *n.* publication
содирот *n.* exports
сол *n.* year
солона *adj.* yearly, annual
сомонӣ *n.* somoni (*monetary unit of Tajikistan*)
сохтан/соз *v.* to build
сохтумон *n.* construction
соя *n.* shadow
сулс *num.* third
супориш додан *v.* to give an order
суруд хондан *v.* to sing
сурудан/саро *v.* to sing
сурх *adj.* red
сухан *n.* word, speech
сӯҳбаткунон *adv.* while conversing

- Т -

таб кардан *v.* to run a fever
табассум кардан *v.* to smile
табассумкунон *adv.* smiling(ly)
таваллуд *n.* birth
таваллуд кардан *v.* to bear, give birth to
таваллуд шудан *v.* to be born
тавонистан/тавон *v.* to be able, can
тавоно *adj.* capable
таг **c.prep.* under, below
тагшин *adj.* coming down, settling
тайёр *adj.* ready
такрор кардан *v.* to repeat
такроран *adv.* repeatedly
тақ-тақ кардан *v.* to knock on (*trans.*)
талаб кардан *v.* to demand
тамом кардан *v.* to finish (*trans.*)
тамом шудан *v.* to end (*intr.*), be finished
тамошо кардан *v.* to watch
танбал *adj.* lazy
тантана *n.* ceremony, festivities
тараф (атроф) *n.* side; **c.prep.* beside
тарафайн *n.* both sides
тарафдор *n.* supporter
тарафи рост **c.prep.* right (side) of
тарафи чап **c.prep.* left (side) of
тариқ *n.* way, route
тарс *n.* fear
тарсидан/тарс *v.* to fear (*intr.*, **аз** *for thing feared*)
тасбеҳ шуморидан/шумор *v.* to count beads
таслим *n.* surrender
ташна *adj.* thirsty
таъйинӣ *adj.* intensive
таърих *n.* history
тез-тез *adv.* often
телефон *n.* telephone
телефончӣ *n.* (telephone) operator
тилло *n.* gold
тиреза *n.* window
то[1] *s.prep.* until; *conj.* so that, in order to

то² (та) *n.* classifier for any noun
то ба *prep.* until
то даме ки *conj.* until, till
то замоне ки *conj.* until, till
то ҳол *adv.* so far, until now
тобистон *n.* summer
ток *n.* grapevine
токзор *n.* vineyard
тоҷик *n.* Tajik (*person*)
тоҷикӣ *adj.* Tajiki, of the Tajiks
ту *pron.* 2*nd* informal *sg:* you
тут *n.* certain mulberry, cottonwood, and related trees
тухм *n.* egg

- У -

уқёнус *n.* ocean
умуман *adv.* in general, overall
уно *pron.* 3*rd pl:* they, them (*coll. for* онҳо)
ура *interj.* hooray!

- Ӯ -

ӯ *pron.* 3*rd sg:* he/him, she/her, it
ӯҳӯ *interj.* a-ha!

- Ф -

фавран *adv.* immediately
фавҷ *n.* troop, host
фавҷ-фавҷ *adv.* troop after troop, in a throng
фалон *pron.* someone, such-and-such a person
фалонӣ *pron.* some person
фалак *n.* world
фан(н) *n.* art, science, field of study

фардо *adv.* tomorrow
Фаронса *n.* France
фаҳм *n.* understanding
фаҳмидан/фаҳм *v.* to understand
феврал *n.* February
феълан *adv.* currently
фикр кардан *v.* to think
филм *n.* movie, film
филҷумла *adv.* as well
фитода *adj.* fallen
фурӯшанда *n.* seller

- Х -

хабар *n.* (piece of) news
хавотир *adj.* worried (**аз** about)
халта *n.* bag, sack
халтача *n.* tote bag
харидан/хар *v.* to buy
харидор *n.* buyer
хаста *adj.* tired (**аз** from)
хашм *n.* anger, wrath
хашмгин *adj.* angry, furious
хеле *adv.* very
хестан/хез *v.* to get up, arise
хишт *n.* brick
хиштин *adj.* brick
хиштрез *n.* brick-maker
хоб *n.* sleep
хоб бурдан *v.* to fall asleep (*trans., direct object indicates sleeper*)
хобидан/хоб *v.* to sleep
хома *n.* pen (*writing*)
хона *n.* house, home
хонагӣ *adj.* of/for the home, domestic
хонашинзан *n.* housewife
хондан/хон *v.* to read
хониш *n.* reading

хоно *adj.* legible
хостан/хоҳ *v.* to want
хотир *n.* memory
хоҳар *n.* younger sister
хоҳиш кардан *v.* to request, wish
хуб *adj.* good (= **нағз**); *interj.* well
худро задан *v.* to make oneself out (**ба** as being/having)
хулоса *intro.part.* in conclusion (= **алқисса**)
хуҷаста *adj.* happy
хушбахтона *intro.part.* fortunately
хушҳолона *adv.* happily
хӯрдан/хӯр *v.* to eat
хӯрданӣ *n.* foodstuffs
хӯрок *n.* meal, food
хӯше *interj.* hush!, shush!, quiet!

- Ҳ -

ҳа *interj.* yes (= **бале, оре**)
ҳабдаҳ *num.* seventeen
ҳабс кардан *v.* to arrest
ҳаводор *n.* fan (*of a team*)
ҳаждаҳ *num.* eighteen
ҳазор *num.* thousand
ҳайфо *interj.* alas!
ҳақиқатан *intro.part.* indeed (= **ба ростӣ, дар воқеъ**)
ҳам *adv.* also, too (*follows noun, see* **низ**); *as prefix:* same
ҳам...ҳам *conj.* both...and
ҳама *pron., adj.* all; everyone
ҳама ҷо *n.* everywhere
ҳамдигар *pron.* each other
ҳамеша *adv.* always
ҳамин *pron., adj.* this one
ҳамин ки *conj.* at the same time that, just as, right as
ҳамин тавр *intro.phr.* so, in the same way (= **ба ҳамин тариқ**)
ҳамон *pron., adj.* that one
ҳамсар *n.* spouse
ҳамсоя *n.* neighbor
ҳамчунин *pron., adj.* (also) this way; *adv.* in this very same way; *intro.part.* also
ҳамчунон *pron., adj.* (also) that way; *adv.* in that very same way
ҳангоми *prep.* during
ҳанӯз *adv.* yet
ҳар *adj., pron.* each
ҳар боре ки *conj.* whenever, every time
ҳар кадом *pron., adj.* everyone
ҳар як *adj.* each and every, every single (one)
ҳаргиз *adv.* never (*with a negative verb*)
ҳарф (ҳуруф) *n.* letter (*of an alphabet*)
ҳарчанд (ки) *conj.* although
ҳарчи *pron.* everything
ҳаст *v.* there is/are (*existential verb*)
ҳафт *num.* seven
ҳафта *n.* week
ҳафтаина *adj.* weekly
ҳафтод *num.* seventy
ҳашт *num.* eight
ҳаштод *num.* eighty
ҳеҷ *adj.* no
ҳеҷ гоҳ *adv.* never (*with a negative verb*)

ҳинду *n.* Hindu, Indian
ҳис кардан *v.* to feel
ҳисса *n.* part
ҳозир *adv.* now
ҳозиракак *adv.* just now, recently
ҳоким (ҳукком) *n.* mayor
ҳол *n.* condition
ҳоло *adv.* now
ҳоппа *interj.* catch!
ҳукумат *n.* government
ҳунар *n.* profession; talent
ҳунарманд *adj.* skillful, clever

- Ч -

чанг *n.* claw
чангак *n.* fork
чанд *adj.* how many, how much?
чандин *adj.* several
чандум *adj.* which? (*of a series*)
чап *n.* left (*direction*)
чаро *adv.* why?
чаро ки *conj.* because
чарх *n.* wheel
чархофалак *n.* merry-go-round, carousel; wheel of fortune
чашидан/чаш *v.* to taste
чашм *n.* eye
чи...чи *conj.* whether…or
чиз *n.* thing
чил *num.* forty
чӣ *pron., adj.* what?
чӣ гуна *adj.* what kind?
чӣ қадар *adv.* how much?; how little!
чӣ навъ *adv.* what kind?
чӣ тавр *adv.* how? (*manner*)
чӣ тарз *adj.* what kind?

чӣ хел *adv., adj.* how? (*condition*)
чой *n.* tea
чор *num.* four
чордаҳ *num.* fourteen
чоршанбе *n.* Wednesday
чоряк *num.* a fourth
чун *conj.* when, as; *prep.* like (*largely literary*)
чунин *adv.* like this, in this way, so; *adj., pron.* such (as this)
чунки *conj.* because
чунон *adv.* like that, in that way, so, thus; *adj., pron.* such (as that)
чӯб *n.* wood
чӯбин *adj.* wooden
чӯбӣ *adj.* wooden

- Ҷ -

ҷавон *adj.* young
ҷамъ гардидан *v.* to be gathered
ҷамъ гаштан *v.* to be collected
ҷанг *n.* battle
ҷанг кардан *v.* to fight
ҷангал *n.* forest
ҷаноб *n.* Mr.
ҷастан~ҷаҳидан/ҷаҳ *v.* to jump, leap
ҷасур *adj.* brave
ҷаҳиш *n.* jump
ҷаҳон *n.* world
ҷо *n.* place
ҷуз *s.prep.* except
ҷузвдон *n.* bag, backpack
ҷумъа *n.* Friday
ҷустуҷӯй *n.* searching
ҷӯйбор *n.* canal
ҷӯш *n.* boiling

- Ш -

шаб *n.* night
шабона *adj.* in the nighttime, during the night, nightly
шабпарак *n.* butterfly
шавқ *n.* love, yearning, desire
шанбе *n.* Saturday
шарм *n.* modesty, shame
шароб *n.* wine
шаст *num.* sixty
шафтолу *n.* peach
шахс (ашхос) *n.* person
шаҳр *n.* city
шаҳриёр *n.* king
шаш *num.* six
шинондан/шинон *v.* to cause to sit, to have someone sit, to seat; to place, to plant
шиносо *adj.* acquainted
шиносойй *n.* acquaintance
шод *adj.* happy
шонздаҳ *num.* sixteen
шох *n.* branch
шояд *adv.* should, might
шубҳа *n.* doubt
шудан/шав *v.* to become; to be suitable
шумо *pron. 2ⁿᵈ pl*: you
Шумо *pron. 2ⁿᵈ sg formal*: you
Шумоён *pron. 2ⁿᵈ pl*: you (N)
шунаво *adj.* capable of hearing
шунидан/шунав *v.* to hear
шӯрбо *n.* a type of soup

- Э -

Эрон *n.* Iran

- Ю -

Юнон *n.* Greece
юрт *n.* yurt (*nomadic tent*)

- Я -

ягон *adj.* some, several
як *num.* one; *adj.* one, a/an
як қадар *adv.* some
як чизи дигар *n.* something else (*instead*)
як-як *adv.* one by one
якдигар *pron.* each other
якҷоя *adv.* together
якшанбе *n.* Sunday
январ *n.* January
ях *n.* ice
ях кардан/бастан *v.* to freeze (*trans.*)
ях шудан *v.* to freeze (*intr.*)

Index

- A -

accusative 12, 17
adjective 10, 26-33, 45
  comparative 27-29
  demonstrative 27, 62, 64
  derived from nouns 29, 37-38
  derived from verbs 12, 69, 71-76
  deverbal 78
  indefinite 26, 117-120
  interrogative 27
  superlative 28-29
adverb 12, 14, 39, 45, 113-120
  denoting frequency 32, 85, 113-114
  indefinite 26, 117-120
  of manner and extent 12, 14, 117
  of place 12, 116-117
  of quantity 14, 117
  of time 12, 14, 113-115
  used to reinforce aspect 81, 82-3, 85-86, 87, 125
  verbal 69, 76-77
agent 95, 96
agentive nouns 36
alphabet 1
anaphora 25
apodosis 141
aspect 69
  continuous 69, 71, 74, 90-81, 82-83, 83-85
  habitual 69, 79, 83-85, 84-85
  imperfect 69
  perfect 69, 86-87, 88-89
  simple/unspecified 69
assimilation 7
auxiliary constructions 127-132
  compulsion 128
  intent 130
  necessity 129
  possibility 128, 129
  preference 129
  uncertainty 127
auxiliary verbs 15, 74, 80, 88, 89-90, 94, 98

- B -

beneficiary 52

- C -

classifier 21
clitics 15
comparative 32, 49, 54
conditionals 93, 141-145
  actual 142-143
  counterfactual 142, 144-145
  doubtful 142-143
  past 142, 143, 144
  possible 142, 142-143
  present-future 142, 143-144
conjunctions 12, 14, 15, 22, 45, 123
  concessive 14
  coordinating 14, 39-40, 123
  of purpose 14
  of similarity 14
  of time 14
  subordinating 123
consonants 2-5
  manner of articulation 3
  place of articulation 3
  unvoiced 3
  voiced 3
copula 55, 56, 105-107
correlative clauses 25, 135-136

- D -

days of the week 116
definiteness 38-39, 40

definite nouns 17, 18, 42, 61–66, 133, 134
deletion 7-8
determiners 27, 28, 33, 38–39
devoicing 3, 6, 7
diminutive nouns 37
direct objects 12, 17, 18, 40, 42, 51, 59, 61–66, 66–68, 70, 95-96, 109, 134

- E -

enclitics 12, 16, 18, 39
evidentiality 69
experiential past 79, 87–88

- F -

finite verb forms 78–98
fractions 30–31

- G -

generic nouns 21, 63

- I -

imperatives 13, 44, 90–91
indefinite nouns 12, 42, 61–66, 63, 133
indirect objects 18, 51–52, 59, 66–68, 70, 95, 109
infinitives 11, 69, 70–71, 71, 78, 100, 125, 130
insertion 8
interjections 15, 122
intransitive verbs 61–62, 96, 110–111
izofat 12, 17, 32, 39–41, 70
   attributive 39–41
   possessive 32, 39–41

- L -

logical object 70, 94
logical subject 70, 95

- M -

measures 21, 31, 32
metathesis 9
modals 98–105
   of ability 98–100
   of desire 71, 100–102
   of obligation and necessity 102–104
   of possibility 104–105
months 116
mood 69
   imperative 69
   indicative 69
   subjunctive 69

- N -

negation 57, 61, 72–73, 75, 76, 80, 81, 82, 83, 86, 90–91, 99, 100, 101-102, 103
non-finite verb forms 70–78
non-specific nouns 64
noun phrases 38–43
nouns 10, 17, 17–22
   compound 33–34
   derived from adjectives 34–36
   deverbal 70, 77
   inanimate 61
   verbal 69
number
   dual 20
numerals 10–11, 24, 29–33, 41
   complex 29–30
   compound 30
   ordinal 32–33

- O -

object clauses 25, 71, 101, 124–127

- P -

participles 11, 69
   future 11, 69, 76, 89

past 11, 69, 71–74, 80, 86, 88, 94–95, 97, 98
present 11, 69, 74–76
particles 14, 121, 122
passives 74, 94–96, 97, 106
past stems 59–61, 71, 78, 89
personal possessive markers 12, 41–42, 45–46, 70–71, 129
  as object markers 66–68
plural
  forms 19-21, 24
  uses 21-22
plurality 21-22, 120
possession 18, 39–40
predicate endings 55–56, 86–87
prefixes 55, 83, 84, 97, 144
prepositional phrases 17, 32, 44–55, 59, 139
prepositions 17, 44–55
  compound (nominal) 46–47
  simple 15, 45, 47, 48–55
  (simple) nominal 45–46
present stems 59–61, 83, 90, 91, 96
principle parts 59–61
proclitics 15
pronouns 11, 13, 17, 22–26
  demonstrative 11, 13, 24–25, 64
  emphatic 44
  indefinite 11, 13, 26–27, 117–120
  interrogative 11, 13, 23–24
  negative (indefinite) 119-120
  personal 22–23, 64
  reciprocal 11, 43, 67–68
  reflexive 43, 67–68
  universal (indefinite) 120
  unspecified (indefinite) 118–120
protasis 141

- R -

recipient 52
relative clauses 64, 75, 123, 133–136, 136
  inclusive/exclusive 133
relative pronouns 133

reportative 13, 69, 88–89, 97–98
respect
  marker of 61
resumptive pronouns 134, 135

- S -

sentences
  complex 123
  compound 73–74, 77, 123, 123–124
  equational 17, 55–57, 105
  existential 17, 56–57, 105
  word order 23, 59, 115, 117, 128–129, 129
specific nouns 64–65
stress 10–16, 68, 72, 78, 80, 83, 86
subject 17, 44, 59, 70, 94, 95
subjunctive 69, 71, 91, 125
  continuous 93
  habitual 93
  perfect 93, 102, 103, 105
  present 80, 91–93, 99, 101, 102, 104, 126, 143
subordinate clauses 70, 123, 136–141
  of place 139
  of purpose 71, 140–141
  of reason 140
  of time 136–139
suffixes 15, 61, 96
  past 78
  present-future 83, 91
syllables 9

- T -

tense 69, 126–127
  future participle 89
  past continuous 82–83
  past distant 88–89, 125
  past imperfect 13, 84–85, 103, 104, 144
  present continuous 80–82
  present-future 83–84

present perfect 13, 86–88, 125
simple future 89–90
simple past 13, 78–80, 84, 88, 125, 143
time 69
  future 69, 83, 89
  past 69, 78–80, 82–83, 84–85
  present 69, 80–81, 83–85
transitive verbs 61–62, 96, 110–111
transitivity 61–66, 110–111

- V -

verbs 59–112
  compound 68, 72, 74, 83, 94
  denominal 60
  of posture 109–110
  of sensing 71, 108–109

prefixed 55, 74
  inseparable 68, 83
  separable 68, 83
  simple 68, 74
  stative 59, 61, 80, 86
voice 69
  active 69
  causative 69, 96–97
  passive 69, 74, 94–96
voicing 2, 3, 7
vowels 1-2
  reduction of 6

- Y -

yoted letters 5–6, 56, 86, 91

www.ingramcontent.com/pod-product-compliance
Ingram Content Group UK Ltd.
Pitfield, Milton Keynes, MK11 3LW, UK
UKHW041919140426
5217IPUK00013B/233